DATE DUE

MAR 16			

GAYLORD PRINTED IN U.S.A

Richard Wagner

TITAN OF MUSIC

IMMORTALS OF MUSIC

Richard Wagner

TITAN OF MUSIC

Monroe Stearns

FRANKLIN WATTS, INC.
575 Lexington Avenue
New York, N.Y. 10022

Jacket photo: Perry Pictures

Library of Congress Catalog Card Number: 69–12391
Printed in the United States of America

For

NANCY and BOB WILLIAMSON

Contents

"His [Wagner's] case was unique in the history of art . . . each of his characters, each of his situations, had been created by the simultaneous functioning within him of a composer's imagination, a dramatist's, a conductor's, a scenic designer's, a mime's. Such a combination had never existed in a single individual before; it has never happened since, and in all probability it will never happen again."

—Ernest Newman

Richard Wagner

TITAN OF MUSIC

• PREFACE

Wagner Today

EVEN during Richard Wagner's lifetime (1813–83) the musical world, including both professionals and laymen, was divided into Wagnerites and anti-Wagnerites.

The first group were those who believed with Wagner himself that his music was not only the greatest ever to be composed but was also the music of the future. They regarded the man as a semidivine genius to be respected, loved, protected from hardship and privation, and spared the responsibilities of lesser souls to moral and financial obligations.

The anti-Wagnerites saw Wagner's music as cacophonous, pretentious, and destructive of much that was beautiful and good in music. They considered him a scoundrel, and his personal life scandalous. Each party was rabid; no compromise or middle ground of opinion seemed possible.

Today, eighty-five years after Wagner's death, the same attitudes exist, but they are far less violent. The anti-Wagnerites seem content with objecting to the undeniably subjective quality of Wagner's music; they prefer either the purer music of an earlier period or the developments of more recent composers. The Wagnerites have generally conceded that Wagner's philosophy is of dubious value today, though they continue to adore his music. Both agree that Wagner's achievement was stupendous.

Furthermore, the general attitude of Europeans should be distinguished from that of Americans. In Europe, all of Wagner's operas, from *Rienzi* (1840) to *Parsifal* (1882), are in the repertory of the major opera companies, and are given splendid productions. Even Wagner's two operas of his apprentice period, *The Fairies* (1833) and *Forbidden Love* (1836), are occasionally presented. And it should be remembered that Europe has many more first-rate opera companies, most of which are state-subsidized, than America, whose few are supported solely by their patrons.

Moreover, the revival of the Bayreuth Festival in 1951, under the direction of Wagner's grandsons, Wolfgang and Wieland Wagner, led to a drastic restudy of the presentation of Wagner's works that resulted in their elaborate staging being simplified to the point of stylization. This modernization made Wagner's principal works much more acceptable to audiences accustomed to the scenic devices of motion pictures and television than was the old-fashioned realistic staging which had come to appear almost ludricrous. Until her death in 1930, Cosima Wagner, and after her, Siegfried and Winifred Wagner, had resolutely insisted on retaining the form and manner of production that Wagner himself had initiated and commanded.

This new manner of presentation has only recently been introduced to the opera houses of the United States. It has not been enthusiastically received here. In America, the old tradition lingers, and has possibly kept new Wagnerites from developing. The present generation tends to prefer listening to recordings of Wagner's music dramas rather than be embarrassed in opera houses by old-fashioned settings, costumes, and styles of acting that are frankly distracting and so hamper their enjoyment of the music. Only *Tristan and Isolde, The Valkyrie,* and *The Mastersingers of Nuremberg,* in approximately that order of frequency, regularly fill America's commercial opera houses. In those music dramas the staging has always been relatively simple.

Another reason for the present decline in the number and quality of Wagnerian productions in America is the lack of singers capable of rendering Wagner's characters acceptably. To do so requires a voice of tremendous volume and endurance, and years of training in both singing and interpretation. The singers of all nationalities who are able to do justice to Wagner are constantly under contract to European companies, and so an American impresario finds it almost impossible to assemble a good cast.

Lastly, the cost of mounting a new production of a Wagner opera in America makes revivals prohibitive without the philanthropy of private persons or of foundations and business concerns. And the cost of operating an opera house in America makes the price of a comfortable seat in one almost equal to the price of an opera album which can be played again and again.

Present-day musical taste in America tends to find many of Wagner's works ponderous. The librettos seem antiquated and often flavored with unpalatable moral preachments. With the exception of *The Mastersingers*, Wagner's works have few light touches, or gaiety, or—and this was Wagner's plan—passages in which a singer can display his vocal agility. The action tends to be slow and is often more of a psychological than a physical nature. The operagoers of today seem to want to go to operas.

Operas, however, are just what Wagner's masterpieces are not. They are, as the text of this book tries to make clear, music dramas. The experience of witnessing one of Wagner's music dramas is, as it always has been, a profoundly moving one. Here are mighty themes expressed in mighty music whose power to excite the emotions no other composer has surpassed. Wagner was the first composer to see that a symphony can be dramatized, and a drama realized in symphonic form. The person who wishes fully to appreciate Wagner's work should approach it as he would, say,

Beethoven's Ninth Symphony, which was Wagner's major inspiration.

The life of Richard Wagner is an epic of courage, determination, and vision. Nevertheless, it contained elements that are sordid, and some actions that are reprehensible. It was alleged during Wagner's lifetime that he was mad, and that only madmen could get along with him. Wagner himself seems to have recognized this factor of his personality; he was fond of the German word *Wahn*. Taken out of context, *Wahn*, like any other word, has no true meaning. It can, perhaps, be defined as "madness," but its real sense is a perception that the things of this world are as nothing compared to the things envisioned by the imagination. Today we are prone to excuse certain actions on the supposition that the perpetrator of them is mad. Wagner demonstrates that such actions can be the glory of human life, raising it—inspiring it, if you will—above the tedium of daily living. Without vision, without a little *Wahn*, the individual and the people perish.

It would be presumptuous for the present writer to claim that this brief biography of Richard Wagner offers any new material about Wagner's life. Ernest Newman's *The Life of Richard Wagner*, the last volume of which was published in 1946, gives and analyzes all the then-known facts about Wagner. Newman, however, was unable to inspect the data in the Burrell Collection of Wagneriana, which was not made public until 1950. Some material from that collection has been included in this work.

Because the stories of Wagner's music dramas are lengthy, it has seemed advisable to the present writer not to include summaries of them in the text of this book itself. The reader will find them in the Appendix. Another reason for placing them there is that Wagner worked on his creations over long periods of time and sometimes set one aside to take up another; consequently the reader might be distracted or even misinformed if the subject matter of the dramas were allowed to interrupt the chronology of the biography. Hence, the reader who is unfamiliar with the stories may wish to read the Appendix first. The works are discussed in the text in connection with the date of their first public performance.

Throughout this text the titles of Wagner's works are given in English, however barbarous the usage may appear to purists. The naming of an opera in a work intended for readers of different language habits from the composer's is far from standardized anyway; English readers are perhaps accustomed to *Don Giovanni*, rather than "Sir John," but hardly to *Die Lustige Witwe* for "The Merry Widow." The German titles, however, are given in the Appendix, where the pronunciation of the characters' German names is indicated.

MONROE STEARNS

RW • CHAPTER ONE

The Mastery of Independence

IN the year 1813 the area known geographically as Germany was perhaps more disorganized politically than at any time during the previous thousand years. The Holy Roman Empire, which once imposed a certain unity on the different peoples and divisions of the region, had finally collapsed seven years earlier. For the 150 years before that, the Empire had been merely an ineffectual remnant of medieval feudalism.

During that century and a half, the states of Germany had been developing their cultural and political individuality. One, Prussia, had become a kingdom independent of the Empire; others, still vaguely loyal to the Empire, had their own rulers—in Bavaria and Saxony, a king; in Weimar and Baden, a grand duke; elsewhere the rulers were princes, dukes, or bishops, and there were also some free city-states. Every one of these more than three hundred political divisions had its own laws, its own machinery of government, and its own army.

The people, however, shared a common language—German—which they spoke in the dialect of their birthplace but wrote in a more or less standard way. Nevertheless, there were cultural differences among the people. For example, most of those who lived in the west around the Rhine River were Roman Catholics. So were the Bavarians in the southeast. The Prussians in the northeast, however, were predominantly Lutheran. The temperaments and customs of the Germans also varied. The Prussians tended to be aggressive, practical, stern, and uncompromising. At the other extreme were the Bavarians and the Rhinelanders, who were inclined to be sentimental, warm, self-indulgent, and peace-loving.

For about forty years before 1813, intellectuals in the several states of Germany had worked to arouse in all the German people a national German feeling. The acknowledged leader of these intellectuals were Weimar's Johann Wolfgang von Goethe, Germany's greatest poet, and his close friend Friedrich von Schiller, a great poet also, but of less breadth of mind than Goethe. Goethe had sparked a revolt against the influence of foreign culture, thereby initiating what came to be known as the early Romantic period (roughly 1773 to 1800). His followers led the later Romantic period (roughly 1815 to 1848), of which Heinrich Heine and E. T. A. Hoffmann are typical.

These poets, novelists, dramatists, and philosophers

struggled to awaken their countrymen to the glory of their history and to the vigor of their ancestors. They strove to revive the independent spirit of an earlier Germany which had successfully resisted domination by non-Germans—the Roman legions, the popes, the Huns, and the Spaniards who had once controlled the Empire. Above all, these nationalists wished to free German thinking from the tyranny of French culture, which they exposed as artificial and effeminate. Imitations of France, they believed, had destroyed Germany's integrity.

In 1813 Germany was more than the intellectual prisoner of France. The armies of the French Emperor Napoleon I had swept victoriously over the region and reduced most of the German states to satellites of France. But in 1812, the failure of Napoleon's invasion of Russia had given his opponents hope that his power could be crushed.

The Germans responded to the urging of their poets and patriots, and determined to fight for their freedom. Prussia and the German states allied with her, together with Russia, Austria, and Sweden, launched a campaign for independence that ended in the decisive Battle of the Nations, fought near Leipzig on October 16–19, 1813. The defeated Napoleon galloped hatless in retreat through the streets of Leipzig. The victory of the allies marked a crisis of modern civilization.

Just after that campaign began, the ninth child* of Johanna Rosina Wagner was born—on May 22, 1813—in the second-floor apartment of Number 3 Auf dem Bruhl ("Swamp Street") in the city of Leipzig. The house, which was replaced in 1886, was named "The Red and White Lion"; it stood behind the present Stadt Leipzig Hotel. On August 16, 1813, in Leipzig's Lutheran St. Thomas' Church, where the great Johann Sebastian Bach had been director of music, the baby was baptized Wilhelm Richard. According to German custom, he was to be called by the second of his Christian names, and to be known to the world as Richard Wagner.

It was an auspicious time for the man who would free German music to be born—much as if an American leader had first seen the light of day between the Battle of Lexington and the Battle of Bunker Hill in 1775. Germany was awakening to a day of independence and unity that would reach its high noon with the establishment of the German Empire in 1870.

Rosina was the wife of Carl Friedrich Wagner, a civil servant in the police department of the Kingdom of Saxony. His title was Actuary; his duties corre-

* Two died in early childhood. Those who survived into maturity were Albert (1799–1874), who became a singer and later a stage manager; Rosalie (1803–37), who became an actress; Carl Julius (1804–62), who became a goldsmith; Luise (1805–72), who became an actress; Clara (1807–75), who became an opera singer; and Ottilie (1811–83).

sponded roughly to those of a modern chief clerk; his salary was 1,045 thalers a year.*

Aside from these facts, not much is known of Carl Friedrich Wagner, except that he was a relatively well educated man for his station in life and that he was fond of the theater. His daughters were named for the heroines of Goethe's and Schiller's dramas and novels. Overwork in dealing with the confusion in Leipzig after the Battle of the Nations made him prone to the typhoid fever that spread through the city, where dead men and dead horses had lain for days in the streets. He died of it on November 22, 1813, having made no impression at all on the six-month-old Richard.

If Rosina Wagner grieved for her late husband or worried over the small amount of money he left, she was soon consoled by the emotional support and financial help of her former lodger Ludwig Geyer. Geyer was an actor and a playwright of considerable ability, and a successful portrait-painter. On August 14, 1814, he married the widow, who shortly thereafter presented him with a daughter, Caecilie.

* Units of currency then in use in Germany were, with their approximate equivalents in present-day American money, as follows:

mark	$0.25
florin	.40
gulden	.50
thaler	.75
ducat	2.35
louis d'or	4.00

In the nineteenth century all these units had a purchasing power about twelve times greater than it would be today.

The household had by that time removed from Leipzig to Dresden, the capital of Saxony, where Geyer was attached to the Royal Court Theater—that is, the company under the jurisdiction of the king of Saxony and somewhat subsidized by him, though managed by an appointee of the king. As a member of this troupe of actors, Geyer had a regular income of 1,040 thalers a year, which he supplemented by executing commissions for portraits. The numerous family he had acquired and enlarged were, therefore, financially secure.

In the rigid social scale of the time, however, they were practically at the bottom. However much the artistic abilities of an actor, a playwright, or a painter may have been admired, his patrons regarded him as little more than a mountebank, probably dishonest, certainly unreliable, and undoubtedly immoral. Women connected with the theater, whether by profession or marriage, were ranked even lower.

Rosina Wagner Geyer was somewhat distressed by these self-righteous moral judgments on the part of the untalented members of Saxon society, and she worried over the possible effect of them on her children. As the wife of a public official in Leipzig she had enjoyed more social prestige. On the other hand, she had absorbed some of the ideals of contemporary philosophers about the equality of human beings, and she believed with them that society would be elevated if only people would make room in their lives for what she termed "the great and the beautiful." This vision she impressed upon her youngest son. She had firm faith in the value of an artist to society.

Rosina was a tiny woman, eccentric but good-tempered, practical as well as idealistic. These contrasts in her attitudes gave her an electric personality. Her children, with the exception of Julius, who seems to have been rather dull-witted, responded to Rosina's electricity and became creative persons themselves. They adored their mother, and they also adored their stepfather.

Ludwig Geyer was a charming man. He had discovered that the illusions which his several professions required him to create were sufficient reward for the realities of a small income and social disdain. He did not need to take refuge behind the flimsy protection of moral hypocrisy. Art was his ideal, and he communicated to his family the joy of the independence they could find in pursuing that ideal.

Geyer was particularly fond of little Richard, whom he called "the Cossack," a nickname suggested by Richard's wild, unruly behavior even when an infant. Geyer loved to roughouse with him and to tell him bedtime stories. Being an actor, Ludwig Geyer so dramatized these tales, which dealt with giants, witches, and wolves as well as with heroes and princesses, that they produced more insomnia than slumber.

Young Richard was deeply impressed by such stories, which Geyer's skill in narration made vivid. He never forgot them. The masterpieces of his later life are derived from the same ancient myths and legends that are the bases of those tales which reveal the main currents of human emotions.

As soon as Richard was old enough, Geyer took him to the theater. From a box the boy could watch the magic of the stage, on which gory melodramas dealing with medieval German life were then the fashion. After the play Richard could be part of the even greater magic of backstage—feel the "velvet" and "ermine" of the costumes, brandish the swords, try on the armor, fondle the "crowns" and "jewels," shake hands with or be kissed by the "brave hero" or the "beautiful princess."

Experiences like those made illusion so real to the boy that he never became fully able to distinguish illusion from reality. Always he firmly believed in the truth of illusion. Facts were to him horrid elements of life to be brushed aside or, if stubborn, to be snuffed out. His world was to be built on dreams.

There were even more experiences with illusion waiting for Richard. When the boy was about five years old, Geyer put him on the stage to replace a professional child actor who was sick. The play was Schiller's *William Tell,* in which his older sister Clara also had a part. Richard was supposed to say, "I'll stay with mother," but when he saw Clara leaving the scene, he would not let go of her skirts and somewhat altered the dramatist's intentions by screaming, "Claire, I'm going with *you!*" The audience loudly applauded his improvement on the psychology of the author.

On another occasion Richard figured as an angel in a tableau to welcome home the king of Saxony. He appeared, he himself said, "sewn up in tights, with wings on my back, in a graceful pose which I had laboriously practiced." As a reward he was given a large iced cake, which he believed was the personal tribute of the king.

After Richard was dead, his stepdaughter recalled that she had heard that he was "a weak, sick child." He himself remembered only one serious "childish ailment," and mentioned his "subsequent good health" as a boy.

It is known, however, that he had weak eyes, which were not corrected by proper spectacles. This faulty vision caused him to see things in distorted form. Stoneware beer jugs, especially in a dim light, appeared to him as gray ghosts, and at night he would not pass alone by the shelf where they were stored. Other objects he saw in both actual and shadowy outlines, as if they had a spectral nature in addition to their real one. One of his common metaphors was "a specter." The defect in his vision made him sensitive, and his sensitivity made him imaginative. His imagination could terrify him as well as enthrall him.

Otherwise he seems to have been a normal boy, active and full of mischief. His chief playmate was his sister Caecilie, whom he dearly loved. Together they would get into plenty of scrapes, for which Richard would invent excuses and explanations that usually averted punishment. Like most boys he was fond of sweets, and ran up a sizable bill for his mother at a pastry shop. Whatever he wanted, particularly if it were to gratify his fastidious tastes, he saw to it that he got. And woe betide anyone who tried to take anything away from him.

Richard's mother and her husband intended the boy to have a career in art. Geyer tried to interest him in drawing and painting, but although Richard liked to mess with Geyer's paints and brushes, he was too bored with drawing lessons to continue them. There were no indications that he was an infant genius like, say, Mozart, either in painting or in music. The perceptive Geyer, however, seemed to glimpse that Richard had more than ordinary abilities.

Before Richard was eight years old he had learned to play the piano. Perhaps Geyer had taught him, and also to sing; Geyer had a good voice which later gave out because of inadequate training, a common mishap among German singers at that time. Geyer loved to hear Richard play, and the last recorded words of that "admirable man," as Richard was to call him, were: "What if he has a talent for music!"

Richard had been sent to school in a nearby village, where he discovered and was fascinated by a biography of Mozart (probably Niemtschek's). He was called home by the news of Geyer's desperate illness. In a neighboring room Richard played the bridal music from Weber's *Der Freischütz* to divert the dying man.

The following morning, September 30, 1821, Rosina told Richard that Ludwig Geyer was dead. "Of you," she added, "he hoped to make something." That evening Richard walked the few miles back to his school with his teacher, of whom he asked many questions about the stars. "I remember," he later wrote, "that for a long time after I used to imagine that something would become of me."

Ludwig Geyer's death meant for the eight-year-old Richard not only the loss of a loving figure of authority but also the loss of a warm, affectionate home. Those losses were a terrible shock to the sensitive, imaginative boy. It was to be nearly forty-five years before he found anything resembling the security he had known in the household of Ludwig Geyer in the Waisenhausgasse ("Orphanage Street"—an ironic name) in Dresden. By that time his resentment of the fate that had orphaned him twice and turned him into a wanderer had made him an almost reprehensible person. But the tragic experience gave him, as a kind of compensation, the emotional drive to transform his personal tragedies into powerful symbols of the tragedy of the human condition.

To ease the strain on his mother, Richard was first sent to live in Eisleben with Geyer's brother, a goldsmith with whom Julius Wagner was also living as an apprentice. A year later Richard went to live with his scholarly uncle, Adolf Wagner, in Leipzig. By early December, 1822, however, he was back with his mother in Dresden and was going to school there under the name, probably for convenience' sake, of Wilhelm Richard Geyer.

At this Kreuzschule ("Holy Cross School") Richard took some piano lessons. He could play by ear whatever he had heard but once, and did so, but his teacher was appalled by the boy's weird fingering and predicted that nothing would come of him. Later, Richard himself said that he had never learned to play the piano properly.

Four years later, Rosina Geyer moved to Prague, where Rosalie Wagner, now an accomplished actress, was performing. Richard, again homeless, was boarded out in Dresden in order to continue his schooling. In that household he discovered the charms of contact with the opposite sex, and had his first love affair. It was quickly followed by another, on a visit to his mother in Prague, with the Pachta girls, with whom he kept up a lengthy acquaintance.

On that same visit during the winter of 1827, Richard made an even more important acquaintance, but a literary one. Already an intense reader, he discovered in Prague the tales of "E. T. A." Hoffmann. This author, who was also a composer and a critic of music, was perhaps the most representative figure of the later Romantic period of German art. The whole tone of that era is reflected in Hoffmann's fiction, which deals in a realistic way with fantastic, grotesque, weird, and supernatural subjects. Hoffmann is largely forgotten today except for the ballet *Coppelia* and the opera *Tales of Hoffmann,* which are based on his stories.

To the fourteen-year-old Richard, already convinced of the "reality" of the spectral world, Hoffmann's work revealed that there was a means by which the meaning of that world of illusion could be effectively communicated to others. The stories colored not only Richard's imagination but his thinking. It was to be many years before he outgrew their tremendous influence upon him—if, indeed, he ever completely did so.

Back in school in Dresden, missing the Pachta girls, his sisters, and his mother, and longing for the old days of going to the theater whenever he wanted, the lonely Richard released his feelings by writing a play about the release of a prisoner from a dungeon and the gory adventures that followed. This *Leubald and Adelaide* combined into one tangled plot all the horrors that Richard had read in the tragedies of Goethe, Schiller, and Shakespeare. To this concoction he added the weird devices of Hoffmann for extra seasoning. The utterly implausible drama contains twenty-two violent deaths.

The family's next move, in June, 1827, was back to Leipzig, where Luise Wagner had found employment as an actress. There Richard saw a great deal of his learned Uncle Adolf, who admired the wide scope of his young nephew's reading and appreciated his quick mind. Encouraged by this attention, Richard showed his uncle *Leubald and Adelaide.*

Uncle Adolf was unimpressed by this fearsome work, and the whole family blamed Richard for having wasted his time at school by writing it. Richard firmly replied that he was not going to let "any school pedantry hamper his free development."

Nonetheless, the family put Richard into Leipzig's St. Nicholas School, where he remained on the rolls—now as Richard Wagner—for two and a half years. But he was seldom in the classes. Luise Wagner could get him theater tickets whenever he wanted them, and after she married and retired from the stage, Rosalie Wagner replaced her in the Leipzig Court Theater company and was equally obliging to her young brother.

Richard also went to many of the orchestral concerts in Leipzig's famous concert hall, the Gewandhaus (literally, "Clothworkers' Hall"). There, on January 17, 1828, he heard for the first time Beethoven's Symphony in A major (No. 7, opus 92). The experience transformed him by demonstrating to him that music is not merely an accessory of drama, as he seems to have thought from hearing operas, but a means of communication—a language—of its own. Its "words" appeared to him as symbols of thought and emotion.

The words of language, of course, are also symbols of thought and emotion, but their effect on the listener is different from that of the "words" of music. The symbols of language can of themselves only describe a situation; it is the sound of them that creates the mood of the situation. Only by *hearing* the words may the sensitive listener approach in his own experience the mood of the writer. The symbols of music, on the other hand, being entirely sound, establish that mood at once. The various sounds of music were, in fact, first called "modes," which is the same as "moods." The listener to these sound-symbols may create for himself the emotional situation that existed in the composer's experience.

To test this real and natural process, the reader is invited to hum to himself, *without thinking of the words*, such widely familiar music as "America," a hymn such as Martin Luther's "A Mighty Fortress," Brahms' "Lullaby," and Schubert's "Serenade." He should find that each one puts him in a patriotic mood, or a reverential one, or a tranquil one, or a romantic one. He acts and thinks accordingly, for a mood or feeling stimulates action and thought. He may therefore understand much better than before what his country means to him, what God's protection means to him, or the bliss of relaxation, or the thrill of love. In that way he has approached the emotional situation of the composer and has achieved relatively complete communication between the composer and himself.

The discovery of this process gave Richard Wagner

an exciting glimpse of the connection between music and drama. He decided that what *Leubald and Adelaide* needed to rescue it from ridicule was music. To learn how to write the music that the emotions of his drama produced in his mind, he rented a textbook on composition from a lending library—and kept it so long that he had to go to his mother for money to pay the fee. Secretly he took lessons in harmony from a violinist in the Leipzig orchestra. Anything to be able to express the emotions of the drama in a better way than by words alone!

Richard stopped his clandestine lessons, which his family had to pay for unwillingly, because he found such technical study boring. "Music," Wagner later wrote of the feelings he had in 1828, "was a spirit, a noble and mythic monster, and any attempt to regulate it seemed to lower it in my eyes." Instead, he learned to write music by copying the scores of Beethoven's Fifth and Ninth Symphonies. Orchestration he seems to have learned from studying the score of Mozart's *Don Giovanni*, one of the greatest of all operas. After he had heard a performance of Mozart's *Requiem* at the Gewandhaus, he lost his previous dislike of Mozart's music as Italianate and effeminate. Mozart and Beethoven were Richard Wagner's masters.

To them should be added Carl Maria von Weber, but less as a master than as a model. Weber had been a frequent guest at the Geyers', and used to do the cooking when he went on picnics with them. Weber's greatest opera, *Der Freischütz,** was the first to use German subject matter, a German scene, and music derived from German folk tunes. Wagner liked it because of the supernatural element in it, and its music had a considerable influence on his own early style. Wagner was a lifelong admirer of Weber's art and of Weber's contribution to the development of a national German music.

Wagner had flung himself so passionately into the world of music that he skipped school for six months. When the school notified his family of his truancy at the end of the summer of 1829, they faced reality and reluctantly gave Richard permission to study music providing he would not neglect his schoolwork. They thought of "music," however, as performing; Richard thought of it as composing. But to please his family he took violin lessons for a short time from young Robert Sipp, a member of the Leipzig orchestra. Sipp outlived him and reported at the age of eighty-three that the then world-famous Richard Wagner had "caught on quickly, but was lazy and unwilling to practice. He was my very worst pupil," the old man added with a burst of laughter.

When the Leipzig Theater, which presented operas as well as dramas, opened for the season of 1829, Wagner's "curiosity," as he called his previous interest in music, "became a more deep-seated and conscious pas-

* The English of this title is "The Freeshooter." It means a hunter who uses magic bullets.

sion." Thus he wrote in his autobiography. This passion reached a peak when he saw the great singing actress Wilhelmine Schroeder-Devrient in Beethoven's only opera, *Fidelio.* Her performance, he later wrote, made the most profound impression on him of all the events of his life. He rushed from the theater, dashed off a wild note of admiration to the artist, left it at her hotel, and "ran out into the night as if . . . mad." When he first met her twelve years later, she repeated that letter to him word for word.

Probably Schroeder-Devrient's thrilling interpretation of the heroic Leonora gave Wagner a clearer vision of a new form of theater, neither drama nor opera (drama set to music) but music drama. In this new form the elements of music and drama would be inseparable, and added to them inseparably would be the intonation, the gestures, and the thinking of the human performer.

Such a tempestuous adolescent was not likely to be particularly studious. Richard's school reports gave him bad marks in conduct, industry, and progress. Probably he spent most of his time trying to master the art of musical composition or in working at his own compositions. He produced an overture in C major, a piano sonata, music for a play that he wrote at the same time that he was writing the words, and, by 1830, a piano transcription of Beethoven's Ninth Symphony.

The difficulty of the music of that symphony and

of Beethoven's late quartets so baffled most musicians of that time that if they were played at all, the performances were wretched. Wagner, however, could read the music with ease and, for his youth, understood Beethoven's intentions remarkably well. Beethoven's introduction of a chorus into the fourth movement of the Ninth Symphony confirmed Wagner's growing belief in the essential unity of music and drama.

By the fall of 1830 Wagner had composed another overture. This one, in B flat major, is Wagner's only work of that period which has survived. Heinrich Dorn, the conductor of the Leipzig theater orchestra, who had become interested in Richard through Rosalie Wagner, agreed to perform it at the Christmas Day, 1830, benefit concert (really a kind of vaudeville) for the poor. At rehearsal, Dorn's musicians begged the conductor to spare them the humiliation of playing Wagner's music, which seemed insane to them, but Dorn insisted. To the audience it seemed less insane than absurd, and they greeted it with howls of laughter. Fortunately for the young composer, Dorn had listed the perpetrator of the overture as "Anonymous," and Wagner himself is said to have laughed.

Probably Wagner's laughter was less at the fiasco of the first public performance of his work and more at the obtuseness of the audience that had failed to appreciate the overture. Richard Wagner could never conceive of anyone being right but himself. Such egoism developed early in him as a result of his discovery for himself of the symbols of music—hardly a world-shaking revelation—and of his vision of music drama. Already he thought of himself as a bringer of good tidings of salvation and release to a world enslaved by antiquated and false ideas. If he was to be scorned and derided, such treatment would be no less than he could expect. He would pay no attention to mockery but would continue to be steadfastly true to his mission. Later he would project his conception of himself as a deliverer into almost all of his dramatic work.

A good deal of his time Wagner also seems to have spent in carousing with the other teen-agers of lively Leipzig. In order to keep up with his crowd of pranksters he determined to enter the University of Leipzig. His school record was no recommendation whatever, but that was no obstacle to the determination of Richard Wagner. Nothing was. He simply enrolled himself on February 23, 1831, as a "second-class student." This rank meant that he could attend lectures (it is doubtful that he ever went to many) but would be ineligible for a degree. At any rate, he was a "student."

Students at that time thought themselves the kings of society in a university town, and acted accordingly. They swaggered through the streets with swords at their side, singing, flirting with the pretty girls or insulting the ill-favored, expecting to be greeted by everyone and never speaking first, revenging fancied insults with cruel or vulgar practical jokes. Shop clerks and apprentices lived in terror of offending them. Professors they liked would be serenaded or cheered half-way through the night; the unpopular ones would be mobbed. Every merchant was expected to give way to the students, for the students knew that the merchants' prosperity largely depended on them. They drank heavily, and fought as many duels as possible in order to get on their cheeks—their bodies, arms, and heads were heavily padded, and their noses shielded—the saber scars that were a great badge of distinction and also certain to win a girl's attention. In 1831 the students were at the height of prestige due to their efforts in suppressing the rebellions of 1830.

These aspects of student life were what attracted Richard Wagner. By 1831, he had probably stopped growing in height, only to find that he was rather short. This disadvantage, plus the need for friendship of the lonely orphan from a low stratum of society, led him into all the excesses of student life. Soon he found himself bound by his rash sense of honor to fight four duels. Fortunately for him, his opponents, for one reason or another, never showed up. Gambling, a common device of the insecure to demonstrate their low opinion of fate, led him to risk all his money and his mother's most recent pension payment as well; he was down to his last penny when his luck changed and he won everything back. He said that this frightening experience kept him from gambling again, but such was not the case. Wagner trusted that luck, or fate, or some other supernatural agency favored him and would sooner or later get him out of his difficulties. True enough, many times in his life it did, always at the eleventh hour. Such rescues did not diminish his egoism.

Like many another egoist, however, Richard loved the luxury of superficial repentance and the comfort of forgiveness. Probably after some unduly excessive student binge, Wagner humbled himself before his exasperated music teacher, Theodor Weinlig, and consented to accept that excellent musician's discipline. Weinlig, the music director of St. Thomas' Church, was a wise instructor. To him belongs the credit for drilling sound technique into his unruly pupil. Weinlig recognized that Wagner's extraordinary musical nature could develop properly only if it was permitted to express itself in its own way first, and be directed later.

After six months' teaching, Weinlig dismissed Wagner in the spring of 1832, saying that he had no more to teach the youth, who had "mastered Independence." Weinlig refused payment for the lessons he had given Richard in harmony and counterpoint.

By March, 1832, Wagner had completed his Symphony in C major. It is a perfectly competent piece of music, but it contains few if any original ideas. Such derivativeness is not astonishing, for Wagner had been intensely studying the symphonies of Mozart and Beethoven. Wagner himself pointed out to the conservative conductor who first performed it (privately, in Prague, in November, 1832) how much the style of his symphony resembled Mozart's; that was the only way he could persuade the conductor to program it. The Leipzig Gewandhaus orchestra performed it on January 10, 1833. The Leipzig press and public liked it. It is the earliest of Wagner's works still in the orchestra repertory, though it is rather infrequently performed today.

A few days after the Gewandhaus concert, Richard went to visit his married brother Albert in Würzburg, about 150 miles away in northwestern Bavaria. The family in Leipzig had apparently decided that it was time Richard did something more about supporting himself than borrowing money. Albert, an important singing actor in the theater of little Würzburg, might be able to do something for Richard in the only field for which his young brother was at all qualified. Furthermore, if Richard were to remain in Leipzig, he might soon be drafted into the army, the last thing in the world he wanted.

So Richard Wagner began his wanderings again.

CHAPTER TWO

Progress and Poverty

ALBERT Wagner found his visitor, whom he scarcely knew, less of a holy terror than letters from the family had led him to expect. He got Richard appointed solo- and chorus-rehearser at the Würzburg Theater, a not very exacting job—the chorus numbered only fifteen—which paid the young composer ten gulden (about five dollars) a month. On the strength of this salary Richard took lodgings for himself and, as usual, incurred several debts.

At the end of April, 1833, the Würzburg Theater closed its season with Giacomo Meyerbeer's opera *Robert the Devil,* which, in the year and a half since its premiere in Paris, had become the most popular opera of the day.

This massive work, a combination of Italian and French operatic styles, was to be for years the standard every composer of opera tried to imitate, if for no other reason than that it earned Meyerbeer a fortune. *Robert the Devil,* which is still in the European repertory, strikes a modern taste as pompous and ridiculous. The plot exceeds the excess of the later Romantic-period dramas in total incredibility, and the music is showy and insincere.

Robert the Devil both impressed and puzzled Richard Wagner, who witnessed it for the first time in the shabby little Würzburg Theater. It was clearly the opera of the present, but hardly that of the future of which he was dreaming. It was successful in that it could not be given often enough to satisfy the popular taste of the time, but it was scarcely the unity of music with drama that Wagner envisioned. Nor was its music of anywhere near the same quality as that of Mozart's *Don Giovanni* or Beethoven's *Fidelio,* the two operas that had so far impressed Wagner the most. To equal Meyerbeer's achievement, however, did not seem to him beyond his powers.

His three months in the Würzburg Theater had given Wagner practical experience in the intricacies of stage production, and in all the intrigues and makeshifts of an opera company. When Albert Wagner left Würzburg for another engagement during the summer, Richard moved into his house in order to complete the opera of his own that he had sketched out before leaving Leipzig. Meyerbeer's example was much in his mind.

During the previous summer in Prague, where he went to visit the Pachta girls, he had written the text and a little of the music for an opera he called *The*

Wedding, but his sister Rosalie had laughed at it and he had destroyed the manuscript. The plot was a gruesome one, derived from medieval romance and E. T. A. Hoffmann, and it reflected Wagner's disappointment in Jenny Pachta, whom he concluded was unworthy of his love. The shoe, however, seems to have been on the other foot; the young lady thought Richard too self-righteously critical of her generosity with her affections.

By the end of the year 1833 Wagner had completed both text and music of *The Fairies.* The story of this opera is also very Hoffmannesque, dealing with otherworldly creatures, magicians, disguises, treason, a gulf of fire, and subterranean chasms. In that respect, and in the fact that Wagner introduced some comic characters, *The Fairies* is not too different from old German *Singspiel* (the ancestor of the modern musical comedy), like Mozart's *The Magic Flute* of 1791. But there is a vast difference between that masterpiece and young Richard Wagner's effort. Like many another inexperienced dramatist, Wagner crammed too much into the plot; even the five acts popular then could not contain the incidents comfortably or intelligibly.

Nevertheless, Rosalie liked *The Fairies* and persuaded the director of the Leipzig theater to accept it. Hoping for an early production in the important Leipzig theater, Richard gave up his job in Würzburg and returned to Leipzig. He left behind him, as he was to do innumerable times in his life, many debts, at least two broken hearts, and a reputation in the theater for being a cantankerous perfectionist.

Germans at that time were good patrons of opera in the sense that they were not at all fussy about the quality of the music they heard or the way in which it was performed or the amateurishness of the production. Music was very much a part of their daily life. Every German who could afford to do so learned to play at least one instrument and to sing. Quartets were formed in almost every family or, at least, in every group of friends. There was no town so small that it did not support a men's choral society or a chamber-music society.

The theaters, however, were social gathering places rather than temples to music and drama. The audiences were too interested in seeing and being seen to pay close attention to what was happening on stage, and a performance had to be startlingly dramatic to capture and hold them. They wanted diversion for their money. The theaters were their only source of such entertainment.

The ideal of Goethe and Schiller that the stage should be an institution to promote public and private morality had little appeal to ticket buyers. The German public took what was good when it was available, but were just as content with a less edifying play or opera.

Goethe had yielded, largely for the sake of financing

his Weimar theater, to the low tastes of his subscribers. Even so, he had resigned his directorship in 1819 rather than allow a trained dog to steal the show on his sacred stage. Richard Wagner was less willing than Goethe to compromise and not willing at all to resign.

When Wagner discovered that the Leipzig theater was not going to produce *The Fairies* after all—it was not produced until 1888, five years after the composer's death—he took to print in a rather naive fashion. In two articles published in 1834, he roundly condemned both the artists and the public of Germany for their low tastes and aspirations. His call for improvement was nothing new, but his determination to realize "new forms" was apparent. His disgust at the carelessness he found in the Würzburg theater had been doubled by the cowardice of the Leipzig theater in shelving his opera. He embarked on a crusade of one to rescue German dramatic and musical art from its slavery to the ignorant, the careless, and the craven.

More or less to get rid of the plaguey young composer, the director of the Leipzig Theater recommended Wagner for the musical directorship of the Magdeburg theatrical troupe. In July, 1834, Richard set out for Lauchstädt, in Prussia, to inspect this company, which was playing a summer engagement at that small watering-place.

On the Saturday on which Wagner arrived in Lauchstädt he found a half-drunk company manager with a slatternly wife, a revolting stage manager, and no orchestra for him to rehearse for the performance of *Don Giovanni* that he was expected to conduct on the following day. Richard immediately decided that this was no job for anyone with his mission to reform the German stage. Politely he said that he needed to go back at once to Leipzig to settle his affairs there. He did not mention that he had no intention of returning to Lauchstädt.

However, he needed a lodging for the night, and a young actor he had known in Würzburg took him to a recommended rooming house. There, in the entrance hall, stood a young and alluring actress, the ingenue of the dilapidated company. If ever there was love at first sight, this was it—at least on Richard Wagner's part. He decided to stay in Lauchstädt after all, and to conduct *Don Giovanni* the next afternoon.

It was the first time Wagner had ever conducted any composition, much less so complicated a work as Mozart's masterpiece. Perhaps his already strong emotional involvement with the young actress made him sympathetic with the amorous Don Giovanni, for the performance came off well. The performers trusted him, and the public liked him, and the ingenue congratulated him, and he stayed on and on. Though his services were repaid only irregularly in money by the insolvent company director, they were compensated for quite adequately by the ingenue's affections.

That young woman's name was Cristine Wilhelmine Planer, but she was known both to the public and to her friends as Minna. She was three and a half years older than Wagner, and had long been supporting herself as well as contributing to the support of her indigent parents. Living with her was a seven-year-old girl named Ernestine Nathalie, who Minna said was her sister, but who was actually her daughter by an army officer named Ernest von Einsiedel.

Minna was an adequate actress, but since she could not sing, she was of limited use to a small theatrical company which gave operas as well as plays and so required its members to be competent in both. Other companies, however, frequently offered Minna engagements, and so it appears that she attracted audiences by something more than her skills on the stage. An 1836 portrait of her is convincing proof of her physical charms.

This definitely second- or third-rate troupe traveled in vans from town to town in addition to playing a regular winter season in Magdeburg, about sixty miles west of Berlin. E. T. A. Hoffmann described the life of his own troupe about this time:

> Wretched lodgings, perilous transportation . . . appalling sanitary conditions in the theaters . . . haphazard and slipshod rehearsals, incongruous scenery, bad lighting, jealousies and indifference, made the underworld of opera almost anywhere a troublous matter. . . . Ignoble salaries had to be supplemented by ignoble resorts.

In such circumstances it is small wonder that the

members of the company led irresponsible lives. No exception was Minna. She had to look out for herself and for her dependents, and she did not wish the always financially embarrassed Richard Wagner taking up her time when there were richer admirers available. Minna was practical.

If Richard had been more practical and less a willing slave to the glamour of the theater, however tawdry, and to his infatuation with Minna, he would have left the Magdeburg troupe. But, as with everything else he wanted, he would not take Minna's noes for an answer. Minna, on the other hand, was, like any other woman, not unflattered by the attentions of the young conductor, whose remarkable abilities were increasing with experience, even such shoddy experience as that with the near-bankrupt company. Life with them was at least a challenge to his perfectionism.

In early February, 1835, after a drunken evening, Richard broke down Minna's defenses. For well over a year thereafter they had a stormy, quarrelsome, on-and-off, intensely passionate connection as an engaged couple. They were, however, often separated because of professional demands on each of them.

The Magdeburg company did go bankrupt in March, 1836. To compensate Wagner for the money of his own that he had spent on a tour to recruit singers, the slippery manager agreed to produce the opera Richard had finished in January—first, on March 29, as a final performance for the disintegrating company, and, on the following night, as a benefit for the composer.

The libretto of this opera, *Forbidden Love,* Wagner had adapted from Shakespeare's *Measure for Measure,* a cynical comedy in which a man pleads with his sister, a novice nun, to yield to the wicked ruler who has condemned the brother to death, and thus save the young man's life. The novice's honor is saved by a trick, and all ends happily. Wagner's music for this story was a deliberate and slavish imitation of the popular Italian composers of the time, Gaetano Donizetti and Vincenzo Bellini.

Those singers who had not already left the foundering company worked hard for their popular young conductor's sake, but they were fundamentally discouraged and tired. At the opening performance, the tenor forgot his part and sang whatever parts of other operas came into his mind. The other singers, without Wagner to sing along with them or shout directions, lost their places in the score. The orchestra members, who had long resented the conductor's fault-finding, took their revenge by playing deafeningly and in any way they wished. The audience, whom the penny-pinching manager had not provided with any synopsis of the complicated action, had no notion whatever of the meaning of the work.

On the next night only three persons showed up for the benefit performance from which Wagner hoped to get enough money to pay off at least some of his creditors so that he could leave Magdeburg. But even before the curtain was scheduled to rise, a backstage fight over the leading lady's affections broke out. The tenor got a bloody nose; the leading lady went into uncontrollable hysterics; the rest of the company took sides, and—the curtain never went up. *Forbidden Love,* the title of which had been changed by the Magdeburg police to *The Novice of Palermo,* which seemed to them more decorous for the Easter season of 1836, was not given again until 1924—and only then as a curiosity.

Unable to leave Magdeburg because of his debts, discouraged by the failure of his opera there and its rejection by the Berlin Theater, and depressed by gruesome incidents he had seen and the loss of his beloved dog, Wagner desperately appealed for help to friends and family. Probably Rosalie Wagner came to his rescue, for by July 7 he was able to get to distant Königsberg, in Prussia (now Kaliningrad, U.S.S.R.), where Minna had found work in the theater and had used her charms to get the manager to hire her lonely lover as musical director. There Richard and Minna were married on November 24, 1836.

Wagner's stay in that outpost of German civilization was a miserable one. His salary was small; he went even deeper into debt for he was being badgered by his former creditors; and the theater was close to bankruptcy. His only friend in the city was a once wealthy opera enthusiast, Abraham Möller, who had a good deal of influence in the theater and so was able to get Richard the directorship of the opera by April, 1837. Wagner disciplined the company and greatly improved its performances, but any satisfaction from that source vanished when, in the following May, Minna ran off with a rich merchant.

Minna and Richard had quarreled a great deal over her friendship with that admirer and also over money matters; but the newlyweds were irrevocably in love with each other, and Minna was the only thing that made life in dreary Königsberg tolerable for her husband.

Richard finally scraped together enough money to go in pursuit of Minna, whom he found at her parents' home in Dresden. They were briefly reunited; then Minna skipped off again with her rich merchant. Wagner decided to divorce her, but for once his determination failed. When, after he had got the post of musical director in Russian Riga, the miserable and penitent Minna returned to him on October 19, 1837, he fully forgave her. But the shameful and humiliating experiences she had caused him poisoned, as he later said, his whole existence.

The stormy life they led more or less together for the next twenty-four years was due principally to the fact that they were temperamentally unsuited, yet irresistibly attracted to each other. Minna had neither the intelligence nor the education to understand what Richard was trying to do with his own music or for music. She craved material comfort and security in the early days of their association and she knew she had to prepare for the bleak days of the future when she would have lost her beauty and with it her career. Her life in the theatrical world of illusion had made her incapable of adjusting to the realities of a poverty-stricken life with a struggling composer and conductor. She nagged Richard about his failure to provide better for her and her daughter Nathalie, thus offending his towering self-esteem and driving him into the violent rages and the intemperate language of which he was capable when frustrated.

On the other hand, Minna remained steadfastly loyal to Richard after her escapade with the merchant. Even before their marriage she had sold a bracelet to help Richard; after her return to him she sold her wedding presents, her costumes, and her jewelry to rescue him from the clutches of his creditors. She did work considered menial in those days in order to keep a home for him.

Richard Wagner was extremely attractive to women both as a young man and as a middle-aged one. He was proud of his easy conquests; they were one of the great supports of his egoism. Like every other egoist, he was ruthlessly selfish, demanding, and inconsiderate. It never occurred to him that he might be difficult to live with. But he craved a home and womanly protection. Repeatedly he would write to Minna, after disagreements had driven them apart, of how much he appreciated the comforts she could provide. And he appreciated her sacrifices for him. Probably each of them was too possessive of self-esteem to subordinate himself and thus make the marriage a happy one. Each doomed himself and the other to misery.

During Richard's pursuit of Minna and her merchant, he had stayed with his sympathetic sister Ottilie and her cultivated husband, Hermann Brockhaus. At their house he had found the latest novel of Edward Bulwer-Lytton, an historical romance of fourteenth-century Rome entitled *Rienzi*, which had been published in 1835.

This epic story of young Cola di Rienzi, who fought to restore Rome from squalor to its ancient grandeur, captured the imagination of Richard Wagner, who was fighting to restore German music and drama to their previous preeminence. Wagner doubtless identified himself with the hero of Bulwer-Lytton's novel, then very popular but now virtually unreadable. At any rate, Wagner immediately saw the possibilities of an opera based on the novel, an opera with a forceful central character; intrigues, plots, battles, and a conflagration; and the background of a colorful era in medieval history, which in Wagner's day was the most admired of all times past. By early April, 1839, two acts of the opera Wagner had conceived were finished.

Wagner's enthusiasm for this grandiose subject made him contemptuous of the trivial fare the manager of the Riga theater insisted he offer the patrons. Hard work and the rigors of the northern climate broke his health. Minna's sister, also an actress, was living with them, and the two prima donnas quarreled incessantly. The manager was not only chasing after Minna himself, but also trying to arrange an affair between her and a rich young Riga merchant. The manager and Wagner became enemies, and finally the conniving manager dismissed him.

Wagner had outgrown the opportunities of petty theaters in the provincial towns of Germany, and knew that he had. Furthermore, he could not go back to Germany from Riga because of the hundreds of creditors waiting to pounce on him there. He therefore resolved to go to Paris, a center of the operatic world. Armed with *Rienzi* and the two other operas he had completed, Wagner was certain that he would be a success in Paris. A major inducement was the fact that the Paris Opera House paid composers royalties on their work, whereas German theaters would only buy operas outright without additional payments to their creator regardless of how often the works were performed. This advantage outweighed such liabilities as Wagner's almost total ignorance of the French language and his lack of any friends whatever in the French capital.

The greatest liability to Wagner's hopes of escape from failure to triumph, however, was the staggering amount of money he owed to tradesmen in Riga, where he had, as always, lived extravagantly. Russian law demanded that all financial obligations be met before a passport could be granted. Knowing this law, Wagner's creditors believed that he could not escape them. Minna, Richard, and Abraham Möller plotted together to elude them. To collect enough money for actual traveling expenses, the pregnant Minna returned to the theater, Richard gave a benefit concert, and they sold their furniture which was not fully paid for anyway.

Abraham Möller got them a coach to the Russian-Prussian border which was heavily guarded by armed sentries. Möller went along with them and their huge Newfoundland dog named Robber, whom Wagner could not bear to leave behind. A coach in those days was an uncomfortable vehicle at best, and the wretched roads made travel in one a continuous series of jolts and jerks. The trip in Möller's crowded, stifling hot coach was well-nigh unbearable for the fugitives.

Near the border, on the second day of their agonizing journey, Möller handed the refugees over to a Prussian friend of his who drove them by back roads to meet a guide. The guide took them to a smugglers' den jammed with other escapees who were apparently criminals. After nightfall the guide led Minna, Richard, and Robber to a steep ditch that marked the frontier at the bottom of a hill. They had to run down that hill, scramble down into the ditch and up the other side, and dash beyond the range of the sentries' rifles—all without making a sound.

Once they were safely across the border, Möller's Prussian friend met them with a carriage which drove them to Möller and safety.

After a few days' rest with Möller they proceeded to the seacoast. Taking back roads to avoid Königsberg and its creditors, the driver lost the way and upset his wagon while turning around in a farmyard. Minna was pinned under the cart. As a result she suffered a miscarriage which, in addition to her other injuries, prevented her from having more children. "I was simply at a loss," wrote Wagner later, "to convey to my poor exhausted wife how extremely I regretted the whole affair." Minna, had she been less loyal, could have got a passport and left Russia by less adventurous means.

Eventually Richard, Minna, and Robber reached Pillau, where they were smuggled aboard a merchant vessel, the *Thetis,* so small that the crew, including the captain, numbered only seven. The three refugees were jammed into a tiny cabin which also contained the ship's brandy cask, so that they seldom had much peace or privacy. They were violently seasick, and to add to his distress Wagner repeatedly had to rescue some seaman from an attack by Robber.

The captain of the *Thetis* was singularly inept. A fearful storm forced him to take refuge in a Norwegian harbor; later he narrowly missed a treacherous reef; and later still, collision with another vessel. It took the

Thetis three and a half weeks to reach the coast of England instead of the usual eight days.

At moments when he was not in terror for his life or heaving with seasickness, Wagner was much impressed with the sea itself, the songs of the sailors, and the Norwegian fishing port of Sandvika, where the *Thetis* had found shelter. But most of all he was fascinated by the sailors' recounting of the legend of the Flying Dutchman who roamed the seas in a spectral ship, unable to land and unable to die, hailing vessels to give their crew letters addressed to people long dead. The story of this ghostly wanderer doomed to homelessness as punishment for a defiant oath to succeed seemed to Richard Wagner almost the story of his own life. It haunted him as the curse haunted the Dutchman.

The travelers spent a week in London to rest and see the sights of the largest city they had ever been in. But there was no theatrical or musical season during that hot August, and so no chance of Wagner's introducing any of his works to the opera or orchestra directors. Consequently the Wagners and Robber crossed to Boulogne, France, on August 20. There they stayed for nearly a month while Meyerbeer, to whom Wagner had got a letter of introduction from a woman he had charmed on the Channel boat, was reading the libretto of *Rienzi* and examining the music Wagner had finished for it.

Meyerbeer, then the great god of opera, pronounced the work promising, and gave Wagner a conventional letter of introduction to the director of the Paris Opéra With this in hand, Wagner, Minna, and Robber set out for Paris, where they arrived on September 17, 1839.

They took rooms in a cheap hotel (now 31 Rue du Pont-Neuf) which pleased the two stagestruck innocents because it was supposed to have been the birthplace of Molière, France's great actor-playwright of the seventeenth century. It was in a shabby quarter of Paris, near the noisy markets, a region of shady reputation.

The place had been found for them by Caecilie Geyer's fiancé, Eduard Avenarius, who was manager of the Paris branch of the Brockhaus publishing firm. (Luise Wagner had married Friedrich Brockhaus, of this firm; and Ottilie Wagner married his younger brother, Hermann.) Once he had done his future brother-in-law this favor, however, Avenarius ignored the Wagners. Probably other members of the family, or his employers, had warned him that help to Richard Wagner could tax the charity of a saint.

Since they knew practically no French, Richard and Minna associated too much for Richard's advantage with other Germans in Paris. Most of them were as poor as the Wagners, and far less talented or aggressive than Richard. They got along on hackwork and on occasional gifts from their families. It was a bohemian circle, much like that of Puccini's starving artists in *La Bohème,* which represents an only slightly earlier period in the artistic life of Paris.

Optimistic and self-confident, Wagner set out to capture the citadel of music in the city that thought itself the most sophisticated of the world. It had not occurred to him that Paris might not welcome a composer and conductor whose reputation had been gained in provincial German cities of which most Parisians had only vaguely heard. Furthermore, they suspected that anything German must somehow be barbarous, and that a German himself was essentially little better than a Hun warrior from the Dark Ages. Mozart had found the same attitudes in Paris some seventy years before.

In the Parisian musical world Mozart was still considered dangerously advanced, and Beethoven's later works incomprehensible. The public appreciated only French and Italian works, and the more trivial these were, the more popular. A progressive composer like Hector Berlioz was almost stifled by the effect on the public of the reactionary policies of King Louis Philippe, a stupid man whose symbol of authority was less the traditional royal scepter than it was the green umbrella he habitually carried. The tone of life in the capital was dull, hypocritical, materialistic, and vulgar. The intellectual vision of social, artistic, and moral freedom that had flourished in an earlier period had faded with the suppression of the revolution of July, 1830.

It was, therefore, hardly a favorable time for a German musician with a passion for reform and an irritating manner of trying to convert the smug to succeed in this environment. The manager and the conductor of the Paris Opéra regarded Wagner's letters of introduction from Meyerbeer with barely concealed amusement; they had seen hundreds like those polite, noncommittal notes. Prominent singers to whom Wagner submitted the light songs he had composed for the popular market saw no reason for risking their reputations on music by an unknown. The established composers were, if not openly hostile to the newcomer, unwilling to jeopardize their security by encouraging him.

One of Wagner's new German friends, however, did introduce him to Moritz (or Maurice) Schlesinger, also a German, who published the *Gazette musicale,* a periodical devoted to musical matters. Schlesinger also published sheet music. Wagner described Schlesinger as a "monstrous person." Certainly the editor did not overpay his compatriot, but Schlesinger did assign Wagner hackwork which kept him and Minna from starving—barely.

The most important of the pieces Wagner wrote for Schlesinger's journal is a short story entitled "A Pilgrimage to Beethoven," which began to appear in the issue of the *Gazette musicale* for November 19, 1840, translated into French from the author's original German. In Paris, Wagner had at last heard a good performance of Beethoven's Ninth Symphony of 1823, the choral section of which seemed to revive his own vision of the unification of words and music into music drama. Beethoven, Wagner wrote, had set the music of that last movement to the words of Schiller's "Ode to Joy" because the emotion of the music was so powerful that words were necessary to define it. Music, Wagner wrote, must be "fertilized by poetry." The poetic words of a poetic drama, Wagner explained, are needed to clarify the emotions expressed by the music. The new form Wagner envisioned was to be a continuous flow of melody whose complete emotional meaning could be communicated only through the means of a drama involving genuine human emotions.

In another story for the *Gazette musicale*, "A German Musician's End in Paris," Wagner expressed his musical creed. His dying musician exclaims:

> I believe in God, Mozart, and Beethoven, and likewise in their disciples and followers. I believe in the Holy Ghost and in the truth of a single, indivisible Art. I believe that this Art proceeds from God and lives in the hearts of all enlightened men. I believe that whoever has once savored the exquisite joys of this Art must forever be its devoted servant and can never repudiate it. And I believe that through this Art all men shall be blessed.

By "a single, indivisible Art" Wagner was expressing his conception of music drama. The visible forms of art he meant to be included with the audible ones. When later he achieved his ideal music drama, he made his audience "see" through his music the settings of his dramas, much as Shakespeare's poetry creates the settings for his plays, which were produced in his time without scenery or costumes. Wagner was to create in music a stormy ocean, a flowing river, tongues of flame, a spring night, a summer forest, or the towers and battlements of the abode of the gods—and make them so vivid that realistic stage settings are superfluous.

"A German Musician's End in Paris" also contains some autobiographical material, such as the loss of Wagner's beloved Robber, who had gone off, probably to find better and more regular meals than Minna could manage for him. For the couple were desperately poor.

On the strength of an insincere promise that *Forbidden Love* would be produced at a theater that was already bankrupt, Richard and Minna moved to more respectable lodgings in the Rue du Helder. To pay the rent they had to take in lodgers, one of whom played the flute incessantly. Wagner must have found this habit disconcerting to say the least, for he was trying to finish the music of *Rienzi*. Schlesinger gave him hackwork in the form of making piano arrangements of the very kind of operas Wagner hated most. The Wagners were hungry and homesick, and Minna even had to clean the filth of the Paris streets from their flute-playing lodger's boots.

Wagner begged everyone he knew for a loan, or the extension of a former loan, in order both to keep alive and also to keep the tradesmen from having him sent to jail for debt. At last, in October, 1840, no help having arrived, he was confined to debtor's prison—a kind of "open arrest." He used this unwelcome leisure to finish *Rienzi* and to make a one-act dramatization of the legend of the Flying Dutchman.

A loan from a boyhood friend released Wagner from custody, and he went back to Schlesinger's hackwork. Even so, the apartment at No. 25 Rue du Helder was too expensive for the Wagners. In late April, 1841, they moved to the suburb of Meudon, a flight which Wagner called "from the impossible to the incomprehensible." They had absolutely no money. They used to pick chestnuts from branches overhanging the street in order to have anything to eat. One blazing hot day Wagner walked into Paris, tramped the streets all day trying to raise even five francs (approximately a dollar), and then trudged out to Meudon again—penniless. It was then that Minna resolved to use her charms on the baker and the butcher, and managed at least to get credit from them.

Then Wagner's luck turned, again in the nick of time. On Meyerbeer's recommendation he had sent the completed *Rienzi* to the Dresden Opera in late November, 1840. A further reason for submitting it there was that Wilhelmine Schroeder-Devrient was engaged at the Dresden Opera House, and Wagner was sure that her appearance in his opera, in a part that he had written for her, would guarantee success for the work. In June, 1841, word came from Dresden that *Rienzi* had been accepted and would be premiered at the beginning of the next year.

On top of this first piece of good news in almost two years, Richard sold his one-act drama on the Flying Dutchman for five hundred francs in July.

He had worked out, in May, a three-act treatment of the same subject, and the five hundred francs gave him enough peace of mind to compose the music for it. He finished this music in seven weeks during August and September, 1841; the orchestration was completed by the following December. Then Wagner sent the entire score to Berlin, where Meyerbeer used his influence to get it accepted by the Berlin Opera House two months later.

Meanwhile word had come from Dresden that *Rienzi* could not be produced until the Easter of 1842, and so the Wagners had to spend another freezing winter in Paris, with Richard doing more hackwork for Schlesinger and others. His shoes were without soles, but his tokens of success had changed the attitudes of his prosperous brothers-in-law. On Christmas, 1841, Luise and Friedrich Brockhaus, then living in Paris, sent a goose to the Rue Jacob, where Minna and

Richard were living, with a five hundred franc note in its beak.

Brockhaus also lent Richard money for his return to Germany. On April 7, 1842, Richard and Minna left inhospitable Paris for Dresden to push the production of *Rienzi*, which had again been postponed. They were sorry to leave their bohemian friends, and Minna wept throughout most of the five-day journey by mail coach. But Richard could never afterward speak without bitterness of his wretched, humiliating two and a half years in the city he considered "the bottomless abyss of vulgarity." He blamed his experiences there for much of his later excesses.

RW • CHAPTER THREE

The Making of a Revolutionary

For all his bitter experiences in Paris, once he was again in his homeland, Richard Wagner looked back on the life in the French capital with more affection that he might have thought possible when he quitted that city. Perhaps Paris was no place for a German, but Germany seemed no place for a composer of Wagner's ambition and vision. And after having seen London and Paris, Wagner quickly recognized that Dresden was narrow and provincial.

Although Dresden was the capital of the autocratic kingdom of Saxony, it contained only about seventy thousand inhabitants, and it supported no business or any industry except the local porcelain factory. There were sharp divisions in the social classes. The life of the upper class centered around the court; most of its members were government officials. Those of the middle class who were not tradesmen were civil-service clerks. The workers were slaves of an economic system in which they had no voice. For that matter, none of the people had any say as to the conduct of their government, which was conservative and reactionary. King Friedrich August II and his court were Catholic, but the state was dependent on neighboring Prussia, which was Protestant, and about half the Saxons were Protestants.

The intellectuals of the city, excluded from politics, cultivated poetry and art and kept up with the latest trends in those fields, but they were not creators. Italian opera had been extremely popular with them, and there was a large Italian colony in the city. King Friedrich August, however, liked German music, and had had the great architect Gottfried Semper build a large opera house for German opera. The monumental Renaissance-style of this building contrasted with the light rococo-style of the Zwinger Palace next to it. The two buildings seemed to typify the change occurring in German tastes from an imitation of French and Italian styles to the cultivation of a national tradition.

Wagner's family welcomed him cordially. The prospect of success through his having had two of his operas accepted made them more confident in the future of their ne'er-do-well relative. They offered him an allowance until *Rienzi* might be produced. Richard and Minna estimated that they could subsist on thirty-five thalers a month (about twenty-two dollars).

Minna was in poor health due to the hardships of Paris, and Richard was nervously exhausted by the plans and counterplans, promises and postponements, involved in dealing with bureaucratic theater managements over the productions of his two operas. *Rienzi,* for example, would require 537 new costumes; *The Flying Dutchman* needed elaborate and complicated scenic effects. For a rest, the two went to Teplitz (now Teplice, Czechoslovakia), a popular health resort. On a ramble in the surrounding mountains, Wagner heard a goatherd piping to his flock. At once a scene of the new opera he had been plotting came into his mind. Between June 22 and July 17, 1842, he had completed a scenario for it.

The subject was a blending of two legends of medieval Germany—that of the Venusberg and that of the minstrel Tannhäuser. As a framework for these Wagner chose the Contest of Song at the Wartburg, the castle of Eisenach in Thuringia, which probably took place in 1208. In Paris, Wagner had done a great deal of reading in medieval German literature and history.

The Venusberg legend is based on a primitive myth common, in one form or another, to all European peoples. It represents the loss during the winter months of the youth and beauty associated with spring and summer; Venus (in northern European mythology, Horsa or Freia), the spirit-goddess of youth and beauty and love, dwells in a mountain cave into which she lures mortals who prefer the pleasure of self-gratification to the happiness of social responsibility. At least, that is the interpretation the moralistic nineteenth century wished to give to the myth.

Tannhäuser, the subject of a delightful poem of the fifteenth or sixteenth century, was probably a real person. He was one of the minnesingers (or troubadours, or trouvères, or minstrels), the poets and singers of courtly love, who flourished in the twelfth and thirteenth centuries.

The Contest of Song involved historical personages, such as the most gifted German poet of the Middle Ages, Wolfram von Eschenbach (c.1170–c.1220); the Landgrave Hermann of Thuringia (1190–1217); another well-known poet, Walther von der Vogelweide (c.1160–c.1230); other lesser but nonetheless real poets; and St. Elizabeth (1207–31).

Wagner planned this mixture of material to satisfy every taste of the time. Meyerbeer's highly successful operas, based on history, had supplanted the fantastic, supernatural stories of his predecessors. The literature of the Middle Ages was being rediscovered and reexplored in England, France, and Germany. The mystical faith of the Middle Ages, a major theme of these legends—the Holy Grail, the saints of the time, the spirit of the Crusades—was being revived as a kind of antidote, or possibly an excuse, for the materialism of the mid-nineteenth century that had resulted from the Industrial Revolution. The moral and religious tone of the period seemed to come from a sense of guilt on the part of the newly prosperous nineteenth-century Christians. They liked to believe that they were making up for their wealth and the selfish pleasures it brought them by posing as martyrs to self-denial and as sinners groveling in repentance for possessing what they had no intention of relinquishing.

The myth factor attracted Wagner himself, for a myth represents a universal emotion and therefore is a good subject for music, which is the language of emotion.

The method by which Richard Wagner blended all these elements of myth, legend, and history into a unified story is typical not only of the way his mind had begun to work by the summer of 1842, but also of the creative process of a poet. For with the completion, in the spring of 1843, of the drama of *Tannhäuser* which Wagner developed from the scenario of 1842, he showed himself to be a poet of considerable creativity.

The creative process stems from a need of the artist to externalize an inner tension, that is, a conflict in his own feelings. Wagner found in the sources of *Tannhäuser* a theme of renunciation and redemption. The Tannhäuser he created from those sources has yielded to the temptations of a sensuous, self-indulgent existence in the unreal world of the Venusberg (Wagner's name for the mountain grotto of the goddess of youth and beauty). This experience, however, has not satisfied Tannhäuser; he feels the need of a more contributive life. His conscience, as it were, demands that he take up again the responsibilities of human existence in the real world. Once back in that real world, he recognizes the genuine love of the self-sacrificing Elizabeth. This love compels him to seek forgiveness for his lapse from duty. He finds, however, that such forgiveness and restoration to a respected position in human society is possible for him only if he renounces the temptation to resume the easy, self-indulgent life he once led.

The theme of redemption had appeared in Wagner's version of the Flying Dutchman legend. But he had then not yet conceived of renunciation as another necessary factor of happiness. Without any sacrifice on his own part, the accursed Dutchman is saved by the love of a woman who sacrifices her life for him. Wagner first named this heroine Minna; later he changed her name to Senta.

The advisability of renunciation and the desire for redemption were hardly new themes in philosophy or literature. They had become, however, dominant in German moral thinking of the nineteenth century, largely because of the emphasis Goethe had given them in *Faust* and *Wilhelm Meister*. Goethe preached that renunciation is essential to productivity in life, and that productivity is the only way to redemption.

A simpler way of putting it, perhaps, is that the unselfish person is the constructive and contributive one, motivated by love of humankind and eager to benefit society. Hence, the principle that a life led for others is its own salvation. Selfishness and laziness thus appear as the twin evils of human life that must be controlled in order for the individual to be free and happy. This point of view, it should be added, has been rudely challenged by researches into human psychology, of which the nineteenth century was ignorant.

Wagner had been greatly stirred by Goethe's dramatic poem *Faust*. In 1832, he had composed music for some of the songs in *Faust*, and, in Paris, in 1840, he had written an overture expressing in music the emotions *Faust* had aroused in him. Being a towering egoist, Wagner was tortured by the feeling that he could never surrender himself to such control and discipline as Goethe advised. He felt that this failure might be dooming him as much as the Dutchman's defiance of authority had condemned him to eternal wandering.

Furthermore, Wagner was painfully conscious of the material sacrifices that Minna had made for him in Riga and in Paris. He was also aware of how impossible it was for him to control the forces of his own nature. It was these that drove him into the excesses of self-indulgence that made Minna's life wretched. If only, Wagner seemed to be confessing in his dramatic poems, he could find redeeming love like Senta's (really Minna's) for the Dutchman! If only he, like Tannhäuser, could renounce his sensuous nature!

The two works, *The Flying Dutchman* and *Tannhäuser*, are the release of these desires of their creator. Similarly, all of Wagner's future creative work would represent the accomplishment in a fictitious situation of what he could not accomplish in his own life.

Wagner also seems to have believed that death is the only release from the struggle for happiness. He argues that so long as human beings retain their mortal personalities, men will cling to them. Hence, all but one of Wagner's major works expresses his sense that human existence is a tragedy. The single exception is *The Mastersingers of Nuremberg,* but even that comedy deals with the poignancy of renunciation.

The tragic nature of Wagner's mature music dramas, however, is an ennobling one. His characters die, but they die happy, for they have completed themselves. Such an end Wagner seems, fairly early in his lifetime of seventy years, to have desired for himself. He drove himself relentlessly toward achieving his ideals. Few persons have worked so hard as he, and overcome so many obstacles in order to fulfill their lives.

In the fusion of elements that make up *Tannhäuser,* Wagner saw how the fusion of music and poetic drama that he envisioned could be accomplished. Music could express the hidden thoughts and feelings of characters impersonated by singing actors while those characters were performing visible actions on the stage. The total drama, therefore, would be an integrated conflict of human emotions and aspirations. It would not be merely an arbitrary, nonrealistic series of actions such as constituted the plots of contemporary operas. And in no event would the logical flow of that development from conflict to crisis to resolution be interrupted by a singer who wished to show off his vocal prowess in an irrelevant aria.

By the time its orchestration was completed, on April 15, 1845, *Tannhäuser* was a landmark not only in opera but in theater as well. After *Tannhäuser* there could be no more of the vapid material that had usurped the musical stage since the time of *Don Giovanni* (1787) and *Fidelio* (1805).

Wagner returned from Teplitz to Dresden on July 18, 1842, to coach the principal singers in *Rienzi,* which had been finally scheduled for production on October 20. These performers were Wilhelmine Schroeder-Devrient and the tenor Joseph Aloys Tichatschek, both of whom were the biggest stars in the German operatic world of that time. With them in the leading roles, Wagner could be sure of a packed house and a first-rate performance.

About five thirty on the afternoon of October 20, 1842, Richard Wagner steeled himself to enter the Dresden Opera House. Once inside, he gave one last look at the stage, then crept to the rear of an orchestra box, where he could see but not be seen. At six o'clock the curtain rose on the first act of *Rienzi*. At the end of the act there was thunderous applause, and Wagner was dragged from the trancelike state in which he had experienced the proceedings to the stage to acknowledge the audience's acclamation. But he appeared only long enough for them to see the tip of his nose, then darted back into the wings.

Throughout the second and third acts Wagner kept muttering to himself about the length of the work. There had not been one uninterrupted rehearsal; consequently the performance had never been accurately timed. Fearing that the capacity audience would not stay to the end of the opera, Wagner kept cursing himself: "What an ass I am! What nonsense! I could have written ten operas from all those melodies. Nobody will endure it to the end."

At ten o'clock he stopped the clock above the stage so that no one would notice how late it was getting. Yet when the final curtain fell at eleven thirty, an hour and a half after the scheduled close, only one person, an old man, had left his seat.

That night Minna laid laurel leaves under Richard's bedsheets so that her hero might literally "rest on his laurels." But Richard slept so soundly—perhaps due to an opening-night celebration—that he never noticed the humorous tribute until the next morning. "Oh," he laughed then, "so that was what kept tickling me whenever I moved!"

That same morning of October 21, 1842, Richard Wagner discovered that he was a celebrity. He and Minna, who, as usual, had been starving, received so many invitations that they rarely dined at home twice in a week. *Rienzi* was given over and over again, and people came from as far as Leipzig, sixty miles away, to hear it. Dresden had rarely had such a success before.

It is a little hard now to understand the enormous popularity of *Rienzi* in Dresden in 1842 and in the other German cities that immediately clamored to produce it and continued to offer it frequently for many years. Its music now sounds cheap and flashy; its plot is fantastically complicated; it has so much of the pomposity of Meyerbeer and similar contemporary composers that it seems hardly an original work. Indeed, a wit of the day called Wagner's *Rienzi* "Meyerbeer's best opera."

But to the operagoers of 1842 *Rienzi* was almost daringly different from their standard fare. Wagner's own innovations throughout the rest of his career are what actually killed his first real opera for succeeding generations. In America only the overture to *Rienzi* is performed in orchestral concerts today, and none too often; for years it was played so frequently at band concerts that it became a wearisome cliché.

To capitalize on the success of *Rienzi,* the Dresden Royal Court Theater management pleaded for the production of *The Flying Dutchman.* Since the Berlin Opera would not schedule it before February, Wagner demanded the return of his score. Dresden put it into rehearsal at once, and premiered it on January 2, 1843.

The Flying Dutchman, with its solemn subject, its supernatural overtones, and a small cast of characters, was not the best work to follow the lively pageantry of *Rienzi. The Dutchman* failed to please the Dresden public, and was withdrawn from the repertory of the Royal Court Theater after the fourth performance.

The music of the opera, however, created considerable interest. The opera was soon given many times in other houses. The first of Wagner's works still to hold a place in the modern repertory, it is perhaps more appreciated today than it was in 1843.

The Flying Dutchman is full of the sound and feeling of the northern sea, of the loneliness and longing of seafarers, and of the strong, simple nature of those who go down to the sea in ships. It has a lyricism that is tender and wistful and at the same time dramatic. There are interesting contrasts in the music of the lonely, tragic Dutchman, the visionary Senta, the opportunistic Daland, and the disappointed Erik pleading his earnest devotion. The rousing Sailors' Chorus and the lilting Spinning Chorus have long been popular, and the Steersman's Song is a charming folklore ballad.

The work, however, contains a considerable amount of the Italian style of opera that Wagner had used in *Rienzi*, and a number of the "set pieces"—choruses, arias, ensembles—which he would gradually eliminate from his work. For the first time, however, Wagner employed musical passages called "motifs" to characterize persons, setting, and intentions. For example, the motif of "redemption," which first occurs in the overture to *The Flying Dutchman*, underlines the motivation of the plot.

The overture itself, though patterned on those of Weber, was another innovation in that it is related to the music of the opera and sets the tone of the opera. Most overtures of the period were independent compositions played to capture the attention of the noisy audience and get them settled into their seats before the curtain rose.

Another of Wagner's innovations was the fact that the principal characters have far more psychological depth than any others had had since Mozart's and Beethoven's. Nevertheless, the emotions of the characters seem a little too arbitrary for *The Flying Dutchman* to be so moving an experience as Wagner's more mature operas, in which he was dealing with elemental feelings.

The comparative failure of *The Flying Dutchman* did not alter the conviction of the management of the Dresden Theater that they should hang on to Richard Wagner and his work. In rehearsing *The Dutchman* he had shown a genius for staging as well as for conducting. He had boldly pointed out weaknesses in the organization and had firmly insisted on reforms, particularly in the composition and performance of the orchestra. Consequently the management offered Wagner the conductorship of the opera house with life tenure and a salary of fifteen hundred thalers (about $1,425) a year.

The position carried considerable prestige, and Wagner had been chosen for it over several more experienced candidates. Yet in spite of his financial insecurity, Wagner hesitated to accept the post. He had already seen how the bureaucracy of theater management could stifle progress in general and his own freedom in particular. He knew that his duties would greatly interfere with his own creative work, and he dreaded the thought of being confined in a city, especially after having found the rural environment of Teplitz so stimulating.

Minna seems to have talked Richard into accepting the offer. She envied the title of "Madame Royal Conductor" that would be hers. She was tired of grinding poverty and hardship and wandering. She had many friends in Dresden and loved the idea of being settled there permanently and prosperously. In deference to Minna's wishes, and in one of his rare moments of self-denial, Richard accepted the appointment, and took up his new duties on February 2, 1843.

Immediately Wagner went about the reforms he had announced were necessary. The chief of these was to make the production of opera an integrated affair—orchestra, singers, scenery, costumes, properties, and, above all, acting. If Wagner had had greater height and a better voice, he could have been a superb actor. He strove to communicate this dramatic skill of his to the performers. Most of all he worked to make the singers think and feel, and hence believe, the characterizations implicit in the music of the masters, especially in his own.

Wagner fully believed in the truth of the illusion of the theater; it was the sham he found in particular theaters that made him dislike working in them. He determined to have no more false illusions damage the effect of his art, or of art in general. To him the illusion of art was reality. Life itself he believed to be an imitation of the ideal world of art. Real life had made him a wanderer and would keep him one for many years to come. His only home was art.

This fervent idealism naturally made it impossible for Wagner to accept the responsibilities of everyday life. He and Minna moved into an expensive apartment which he furnished extravagantly. His passion for sensuous luxury plunged him even deeper into debt than he already was. Thanks to the success of his operas, his permanent post as conductor, and the fact that his name was now known throughout Germany, Wagner could get credit. Due to the same factors, however, his creditors, especially his former ones, kept hounding him for payment of their accounts.

The dishonesty of living beyond his means never bothered Richard Wagner. Nor was he ever embarrassed by asking anyone whatever for a loan. Eventually he had to borrow a sizable sum from the Dresden Theater, thus mortgaging his services to it, but the morality of that obligation troubled him not at all. The only responsibility he honored was his duty to his own art and to the art of the composers whose music he undertook to render. Immorality to Wagner was failure to realize their intentions as fully as possible.

In that respect, Wagner labored as hard and as enthusiastically for other music he respected as he did for his own. He was able to bring to the interpretation of masters like Gluck, Mozart, and Beethoven the intuitive sense of their intentions that only an equally gifted composer could give. He sensed the total meaning of a work rather than merely what the notes said. Consequently he developed a then new style of conducting—playing the music according to phrase rather than by measure, and varying the tempo in order to give the phrases an emotional significance.

For a famous performance of Beethoven's Ninth Symphony, Wagner rehearsed the cellos and bass viols twelve times in a single passage. He drove the choir relentlessly until he had forced into them his own feeling of jubilation and made them sing the "Ode to Joy" with some sense of the exaltation Beethoven himself might have had.

For a new production of Gluck's *Iphigenia in Aulis,* Wagner restudied the original score, restored Gluck's tempos, and stripped the opera of "improvements" with which other conductors had defaced it. Then he integrated the choruses and the arias, coached the singers in both singing and acting, and staged the work as well as conducting it—a herculean labor far beyond Wagner's contractual obligations.

For the first few years in Dresden, the management of the theater and the public were entirely on Wagner's side. They had hoped for great things from him, and they were gratified by the results he obtained. The management was generous in granting him vacations, and during them he worked at completing *Tannhäuser.*

While he was working on *Tannhäuser,* however, Wagner could not escape the feeling that it would not express all he wished. It was too late for him to abandon it, even if he had wanted to do so, but it was not too late for his furiously active imagination to conceive another work which might bring him nearer to his ideal.

The subject for this work returned to Wagner's mind from the intensive reading in ancient German literature which he had done in Paris. It was the Knight of the Swan, or Lohengrin, who appears in various guises in many old legends. The story attracted Wagner again in 1844, not only because of its basis in German folklore and myth, but also because it represented Wagner's own feeling that he was a mystical savior from a mysterious land (the visionary world of his imagination) come to rescue and redeem a noble soul (German art) unjustly held captive.

By November, 1845, Wagner was reading the dramatic poem he had made out of the Lohengrin legends to some friends. This custom he insisted upon inflicting on one group or another; it must have been tedious for them because Wagner had a nasal voice and a slight lisp. In the meantime, on his summer holiday of 1845, Wagner had sketched the libretto of *The Mastersingers,* based on another subject from medieval German history and with another theme of renunciation, this time for the sake of art.

Tannhäuser was produced in Dresden on October 19, 1845. The performance disappointed Wagner. In rehearsals he had failed to get the singers to think through the characters and to conceive of his new style of music as "endless melody," as he termed it.

The new scenery had not arrived in time for the premiere. Wagner himself had directed the final scene in such a way that the motivations of the characters were incomprehensible to the audience. These spectators, puzzled enough by Wagner's unorthodox music and by familiar settings from another opera, were baffled by the ending. The critics confirmed the public's confusion as to Wagner's intentions.

A second performance, with cuts and with appropriate scenery, drew only a small house. Word spread, however, that the opera was not so bad as had been thought. The pageantry of the work had been noticed; its elevating theme was appreciated by those in the audience who felt guilty over their own shortcomings; and the sharp contrasts in settings, characters, and mood pleased a public accustomed to melodrama. By November 2, the opera house was full for the fourth performance. Thereafter *Tannhäuser* was a success.

The music of *Tannhäuser* that is heard today contains the revisions Wagner made in the original score fifteen years after the first production. By that time he was a mature composer with such masterpieces of music drama as *The Valkyrie* and *Tristan and Isolde* behind him. He also gave the characters more plausible motivations. The opening scene in the grotto of Venus is now a superb piece of sensuous music. If that scene is imaginatively staged, if the Venus is visibly credible, and if the exotic dancing of her nymphs and satyrs is alluringly executed, a modern audience might question the sanity of Tannhäuser in forsaking such a paradise for the torments of earthly trials.

Consequently, the rest of the opera, noble though much of the music is, strikes the modern mind as "preachy." It is a period piece, smelling of the mothballs of mid-nineteenth-century morality which now appears to have been rather hypocritical. The "Pilgrims' Chorus" and the "Song to the Evening Star" will probably always hold considerable appeal, perhaps justifiably, but there are too many other passages of lamentable sentimentality or just plain mediocre writing for *Tannhäuser* to be ranked as a truly great opera.

The two and a half years following the premiere of *Tannhäuser* were full of overwhelming mental and spiritual turmoil for Wagner. *Tannhäuser* had not brought him close enough to his ideal of music drama to satisfy him. Advanced as that opera was, it still had too many of the standard "numbers" and "scenes" of traditional opera for the complete integration he wanted. The music showed the characters in action, but not in *inter*action. It was not yet "endless melody," progressing without interruption from logical premise to logical conclusion. The motifs, Wagner recognized, should not have been used merely to recall a situation; in the future he must use them in constant repetition to represent the continuing emotions of the characters as those developed in logical sequence from conflict to resolution.

In Dresden, Wagner found no one who could understand such revolutionary ideas. In addition, the bureaucratic management of the theater was almost daily becoming more and more critical of Wagner's demands for improvements. These demands were utterly logical, but they were also revolutionary, and neither logic nor change for the better has ever been understood or appreciated by bureaucrats. Neither are bureaucrats likely to appreciate an intemperate manner when demands are made, and Wagner was prone to be offensively tactless. Lastly, the clamor of Wagner's creditors had made him feel abused and persecuted.

As a result of this lack of understanding, Wagner felt lonely and isolated. Supreme egoist that he was, he believed that his dedication to art entitled him to everyone's complete faith in his mission and to the immediate and complete granting of his smallest request. These conflicts made him physically ill with digestive troubles which would plague him for the rest of his life. Wagner's fondness for high living, now that he could get credit, originated these digestive complaints, but his mental struggles doubtless aggravated them.

In the summer of 1846 Wagner retired to the country for the sake of his health, and began the music of *Lohengrin*, the poem of which he had finished at a health resort the previous summer. Into the musical portrait of the Swan Knight he poured all the loneliness and isolation and distrust by others of his motives that he himself felt. The rest of the story he stripped to its essentials so that the mystical mood of the music would not be hampered by the distraction of details. Wagner was aiming at music that would express what he called "purely-human emotion." That is why he had turned to legend for his subject matter; he would not have to respect historical detail. Now he wanted to simplify legend to myth, which represents universal emotions. Reduced to this basic level of communication, the simple situations of his story could be expressed by music that would convey the emotions implicit in them.

The score of *Lohengrin* was finished by the end of March, 1848. By that time, Wagner had moved out of Dresden proper to a suburb. The move was a symbol of his rejection of the policies of the Dresden Theater in retaliation for its rejection of his plans. He had become obsessed with the idea of a rebirth of German civilization through a new national attitude toward the theater, and had written a long report to the authorities on the reforms he thought necessary to bring this about. When this report was turned down, Wagner became convinced that nothing short of a political revolution could make possible the improvements upon which he had set his heart and for which he was ready to risk his soul.

In February, 1848, revolution had broken out in Paris, led by liberals who demanded political democracy with universal male suffrage, and economic democracy guaranteeing the right to work. The revolutionary spirit quickly spread to Germany. By March, there were barricades in the streets of Berlin, and more than two hundred workingmen were killed in the rioting. In March, 1849, a national constitutional convention in Frankfurt completed the draft of a liberal document providing for a federal government in Germany to which the individual states would surrender much of their power. This representative government would speak for the people against the autocratic rulers, whose oppression could thus be controlled.

The intellectuals of Germany supported the liberals in the hope that their dreams of an ideal state, including a national theater, would come true through the emancipation of the people from autocracy and its servant bureaucracy. Wagner spent two months in the spring of 1848 drawing up a *Plan for the Organization of a German National Theater for the Kingdom of Saxony.*

By presenting this commonsensical program directly

to the politicians in the Saxon government, Wagner went over the head of the director of the Dresden Theater and greatly antagonized him. The director could see only that Wagner was trying to oust him and all other political appointees in the theater. The politicians were too busy saving their own skins to worry about a matter so inconsequential to them as a national theater.

The result of his idealistic efforts was that Wagner now had a host of enemies and no protection or help from the government authorities. *Lohengrin* was rejected by the theater, and the scheduled revival of *The Flying Dutchman* was canceled. Wagner was not permitted to conduct the 1848–49 season of orchestral concerts.

Revolution now seemed the only hope for Wagner's own works and for his projects. In early 1849 he began contributing articles to a revolutionary weekly journal, in which he agitated for a national theater. Since he was still a government employee, this action was little short of treason. Consequently he was closely watched because of his association with well-known revolutionaries, among whom was Mikhail Bakunin, one of the real founders of communism.

On Thursday, May 3, 1849, Wagner was present at a meeting of a revolutionary organization. A resolution was passed to offer armed resistance to the conservative government which had dissolved the representative legislature of Saxony three days previously for demanding recognition of the Frankfurt Constitution. The city of Dresden was seething with excitement and full of rumors about the outbreak of revolution elsewhere in Germany. On Wagner's way home, about three o'clock on that sunny afternoon, the church bells began to ring, signaling the beginning of a rebellion. The exasperated workers had attacked the city arsenal, and five civilians had been killed by the soldiers who were defending it.

The cry of "To the barricades!" swept through the city. Wagner joined the crowds rushing to the Town Hall, the center of the revolutionists.

From that moment on, until the revolt was put down on the morning of May 10, Richard Wagner was in the thick of it. He borrowed guns for the insurgents from Tichatschek's collection while the tenor was absent from his house. He had placards printed urging the Saxon City Guard to remain loyal to their fellow citizens against the Prussian troops that had been sent to quell the rebellion. He was present in the Town Hall for the forming of a provisional government. He stood watch all one night on a church tower which was the rebels' principal observation post. He went whereever the revolutionary leaders went, and was present at their policy meetings.

When the rebellion collapsed as the foreign troops closed in on the Dresden insurgents, Wagner jumped into a coach and fled for safety to his brother-in-law's house in a suburb.

Bakunin and other revolutionary leaders followed him, hoping to reorganize the insurrection outside the city. They were arrested, tried, and sentenced to death. Somehow fate saw to it that Richard Wagner was overlooked in that police raid.

RW • CHAPTER FOUR

Illusions of Refuge

FAMILY loyalty on the part of Richard Wagner's sister Clara and her husband Heinrich Wolfram did not extend to giving refuge to a defeated leader of the rebellion who was wanted by the police. Minna was, on the one hand, furious with Richard for having deprived her of security and social prestige, and, on the other hand, frantic with anxiety over his safety. She managed to stall off the pursuing police while Heinrich Wolfram got Richard out of the suburb by coach in the dead of night.

The basic differences between the motivations of Minna and Richard had already divided them more than the mere miles that were to separate them for the next few months. Minna was content to fit into any environment successfully. Richard's drive was toward creative expansion—influence, power, and the production of works he would leave to posterity. Richard resented Minna's inability to believe in his ideals, and especially her failure to go along with his revolutionary activities. Her continual reproaches to him for endangering her security made Richard feel alone even in his own home. Yet he had recently written her from Berlin, where he had gone to arrange for productions of his operas: "What is a young passion compared to a *love* like ours? . . . For real enjoyment take a love like ours. A brief separation makes that perfectly plain—though Heaven preserve us from a long one, eh, old girl?"

Once again Richard Wagner became a solitary wanderer. This time, however, he felt less regret at being an exile than joy in being free from the harassments he had experienced in Dresden at the hands of the bureaucrats and, perhaps, of Minna as well. He headed ninety miles west to Weimar, the capital of the Grand Duchy of Saxe-Weimar-Eisenach, where he trusted that Franz Liszt would give him refuge. He arrived on May 13, 1849.

Wagner had met Liszt twice in Paris. At that time Liszt's success as the most brilliant piano virtuoso of the era had made the struggling, starving Richard Wagner bitterly envious. Liszt had treated Wagner politely, but had showed no real interest in him. Liszt, however, had come to Dresden in 1844 to witness *Rienzi*, and had been greatly impressed by it. From then on, being dedicated to progress in music, Liszt had sung Wagner's praises wherever he went on his triumphal tours as a concert pianist. The two men became close friends, and Wagner depended a great deal on Liszt's influence with officials in the musical world.

At that time Liszt was the only major musician in Europe who befriended Wagner. Mendelssohn and Schumann condemned Wagner's innovations in music as destructive of the classical style they championed; Meyerbeer was envious of Wagner after the success of *Rienzi*, and, out of fear that he might be supplanted by the younger man, was becoming hostile.

Franz Liszt was a sensuous man who had been and was yet to be involved in many romantic affairs. He was also a profoundly religious man who would eventually enter the Roman Catholic Church as a secular priest. Not yet a distinguished composer, he was nonetheless already beginning to produce the long list of works for orchestra or piano, the merit of which is still a matter of controversy. Today probably the best known and most frequently performed of Liszt's works are his "Hungarian Rhapsodies" and "Les Préludes."

In 1848 Liszt was appointed director of music to the ducal court at Weimar. Resolving to restore Weimar to the position of leadership it had held in the great days of Goethe and Schiller thirty-five years before, Liszt almost abandoned his concertizing and devoted himself to producing new music in Weimar and to helping fellow musicians.

Liszt welcomed Wagner to Weimar, and they immediately planned productions of *Tannhäuser* and the still unperformed *Lohengrin* for the Court Theater there. *Lohengrin* was given its first performance, with Liszt conducting, in Weimar on August 28, 1850, but Wagner did not attend; indeed, he never saw this work performed until 1861.

For it soon became clear that Weimar could not remain on good diplomatic terms with Saxony and continue to harbor a man who now had been declared a political exile from Saxony and for whom a warrant of arrest had been circulated. Wagner could have returned to Dresden, and probably even wanted to return. The king of Saxony wanted him back; Wagner had had no quarrel with the king or with royalty as an institution, only with the ministries. The warrant was loosely worded. Wagner would not, however, perform the political act of contrition that was required of him before he could be reinstated as a Saxon citizen and as *royal conductor*. Instead, he resolved to get out of Germany.

Before leaving Weimar, Richard insisted on seeing Minna again. In disguise and with a false passport he met her at Jena, twelve miles from Weimar. The reunion was probably unpleasant. Minna, Wagner later wrote, "persisted in regarding me as an ill-advised, inconsiderate person who had plunged both of us into the most terrible situation." But at the time, they seemed to cling to their love for each other. Minna insisted that Richard should leave Germany for the sake of his safety, though she refused to go into exile with him. Richard was sincerely concerned over what her welfare would be in his absence.

That night, May 24, Wagner set out for a refuge in neutral Switzerland, and crossed the border, again with a false passport, on May 28. From there he wrote Minna very affectionately that he was safe.

Eventually Wagner settled in Zürich. That city of thirty thousand inhabitants, at the head of a lovely lake, pleased him, and the mountain scenery of its environs seemed to promise him the freedom he had fought for. He urged Minna to join him there, predicting that they could lead a happy, carefree life together in Switzerland.

Minna, however, had no wish to leave Dresden for provincial Zürich. She even proposed a permanent separation. She could not comprehend Richard's needs as an artist, two of which were her herself and the comfort of the home she could make for him.

At last Minna did reluctantly consent to join him in Zürich after he had promised to write an opera for production in Paris and make some money thereby. At the end of August, 1849, she arrived with the dog Peps and the parrot Papo. Both Minna and Richard were devoted to these pets, which took the place of the children they wanted but could not have. Soon Minna was reproaching Richard again for not working at an opera or earning money by any other means.

As usual, Wagner had been living on loans from

friends, including Liszt, who admired his work and were captivated by his magnetic personality. Then, on a trip to Paris with the sketches of two operas he hoped to sell there, Wagner met Jessie Taylor Laussot. This young Englishwoman, unhappily married to a wine merchant of Bordeaux, together with Frau Julie Ritter, the mother of an unstable young musician who worshiped Wagner, offered to support him with an allowance.

Wagner's immediate acceptance of the offer led to an understanding between him and Jessie Laussot which was promptly resented by their respective spouses. Minna swept down on Paris to recapture Richard; Eugène Laussot threatened thrashings and bought a pistol. Richard returned to Zürich and persuaded himself that he had overestimated Jessie's capacities for understanding him. The conclusion to the rather ridiculous episode reunited Richard and Minna in much the same way that Minna's similar escapade some thirteen years earlier had ended in bringing them together again.

The operas Wagner had sketched for possible sale in Paris he quickly abandoned. Instead he turned to writing books which he almost bribed publishers to issue. In these he expounded his revolutionary theories of the art of music.

As a poet Wagner was more than adequate; as a writer of expository prose he was terrible. His copious prose writings require a great deal of studious attention for his intentions to become more than dim. Many of his meanings are clear at all only when one goes from his music dramas themselves back to his theories about them. As a creator Wagner was superb; as an analyst, he only made matters more complicated.

At the bottom of these theories lies Wagner's vision of an atmosphere to be realized in the Germany of his own day similar to that of the Athenians in the Golden Age of Pericles in the fifth century before Christ. Then the great dramas of Sophocles, Aeschylus, and Euripides were presented as religious ceremonials lasting all day for days at a time, and the Greeks were obliged to attend them. Free tickets were supplied by the government to those citizens who could not pay the price of admission. Wagner's dream of a national German theater followed that Greek model. His own music dramas were to be the nineteenth-century counterpart of the cycles of the Greek tragedians.

Wagner's knowledge of Greek drama, however, and especially of the actual life and attitudes of Periclean Athens was limited. He was not aware, for example, that the audiences at the Greek festivals may have been captive ones by law but not all the members were enthralled by the state policy of compulsory culture or willing to give the programs the intense concentration Wagner demanded for his own works. Also, it seems not to have occurred to Wagner that a single Greek drama requires no more than an hour for performance, whereas his music dramas average more than one hour per act. Nor did Wagner's egoism permit him to see that there might be a difference between life among the Germans of the mid-nineteenth century, already speeded up by railways and the telegraph, and life in leisurely Athens some twenty-two centuries earlier.

Nevertheless, as early as September 20, 1850, Wagner had conceived of a four-day national festival of music drama on each of which days one part of a four-part cycle, or tetralogy, to be written by Wagner himself, was to be presented. Only by such an institution could the German "folk" be spiritually ennobled as were the glorious Greeks of the age of Pericles. "Folk" was Wagner's word for those Germans who he thought shared a common spirit of "high-souled dreams and deep-brained thought."

This imaginary notion of the inner nature of the German nation, which did not yet exist even as a political fact, led Wagner into the perverted foolishness of denouncing all groups who he thought did not share it. His egoistic faith in his own ideas blinded him to logic and reality.

Wagner's longest prose work of theory, *Opera and Drama,* published on February 16, 1851, contains a great deal of gobbledygook about language, but does state what he intended in music drama. The language of his dramas would be a continuous wave of melody in itself, for the emotions it would express are continuous. Under that wave would be currents—the underlying issues of the drama. These were to be expressed by the obviously nonspeaking orchestra. The issues thus would become motifs continuously rendered by the orchestra to communicate the feeling or mood of the drama. Thus they would add a new dimension to opera form.

To put these theories into practice, and also to fulfill Liszt's helpful advance payment for an opera to be composed for Weimar, Wagner decided in 1851 to expand "The Death of Siegfried," the poem of which he had finished on November 28, 1848. Essentially this poetic drama is the same as the present libretto of *The Twilight of the Gods*. Wagner now saw that for its action to be understood, he would have to preface it with material dealing with preceding events in the life of Siegfried, the hero of the Nibelungen saga, from which ancient folk poem he had derived the story of "The Death of Siegfried."

In 1847, while he was still working on *Lohengrin*, Wagner had decided that myth was to be the subject matter of all his future "poetic stuff." By that term he meant dramas dealing with the heroic figures of long ago. Such mythical personages, by the very nature of myth, would demonstrate basic human emotions because their stories were not cluttered up with the complexities of more modern times. Nor would he need to respect historical accuracy, because the world of myth is a timeless one. Even in the stripped-down story of *Lohengrin* he had felt limited by the politics of its king, Henry the Fowler (919–36). With this new subject matter of ancient myth, he would be utterly free in his approach.

Also about the same time (1847) Wagner seems to have determined that his "poetic stuff" should in the future merely define the emotions expressed by the music. The music was to supply the emotional power; the "poetic stuff" was to direct that power into the mind of the listener. The result would, therefore, be a union of feeling and thinking that would affect those two factors in the personalities of Wagner's audiences. The simpler the subject matter, the more powerful would be the music's emotional appeal through it.

In 1847 and 1848, when Wagner was mentally and spiritually depressed and overwhelmed by the loneliness of his intellectual existence, the mythical Siegfried appeared to him as an almost perfect projection of his own state of mind. Lohengrin, the character he was actually creating then, was taking form as a misunderstood and doubted rescuer. Siegfried, however, another noble hero, was to be destroyed by the ignoble world he was created to redeem.

At about the same time Wagner also projected a music drama about Jesus, the greatest of all despised, rejected, and destroyed saviors sent into an evil world to save it. Fortunately, Liszt, who had a certain sense of humor, seems to have talked Wagner out of continuing that project.

By June 24, 1851, Wagner had completed the drama

of "Young Siegfried," essentially the same as the libretto for the *Siegfried* of today. But Wagner doubted the wisdom of giving it to Liszt for a Weimar production. Reports of Liszt's mounting of *Lohengrin* had persuaded Wagner that Liszt might have done all he could for that opera, but that his resources were inadequate. Furthermore, in spite of Liszt's efforts, Weimar was of very little importance in the musical world of Germany.

"Young Siegfried" demonstrated to Wagner that still more explanatory material should precede it in order for him to make his mythical hero's relationship to the unheroic world completely comprehensible. In the autumn of 1851, Wagner wrote in a letter that he had in his head "some big plans besides 'Young Siegfried'—three dramas, plus a three-act Prologue." "If all the German theaters tumble down," he added, "I will erect a new one on the banks of the Rhine, call people together, and produce the whole in the course of a week."

A few weeks later, Wagner asked a Dresden friend to smuggle out of the Royal Library one of the source books of the Siegfried myth. He was, he said, already so far along in his work of expanding the legend that he could send his friend an outline of the next two dramas he would base upon it.

Wagner was now embarked upon the twenty-six-year (1848–76) project of the tetralogy of music drama he envisioned as a reproduction of the ancient Athenian religious festivals of drama. It would express and thus reawaken the fundamental spirit of the German "folk," purify that spirit of the base elements that had corrupted it, and ennoble the nation and make it superior to all other nations of the world.

The completed project, *The Ring of the Nibelungs*, as the cycle was to be titled, is one of the most stupendous achievements ever contemplated and executed by one man. Not only that, but Wagner's untiring efforts to produce it as he dreamed of doing, and which culminated in the Bayreuth Festival of 1876, is as astonishing as the mythical twelve labors of the hero Hercules.

Wagner was so sure that the mighty project he had begun was the only way by which he could satisfy his inner drives that he borrowed money to repay Liszt's advance on an opera for Weimar. Gone were Liszt's hopes for a new opera in the near future, and with them went a considerable amount of the influence Liszt had had on Wagner. Luckily for Wagner, Julie Ritter, in November, 1851, offered to continue Wagner's yearly allowance herself, at a slightly lower figure than when Jessie Laussot was contributing to it.

The Flying Dutchman was given four times by the Zürich Opera House in 1852, bringing Wagner some money, as did the subscription concerts he conducted for the Zürich orchestra beginning in 1851. At one of these Wagner conducted Beethoven's Symphony in F major (No. 8, opus 93) so persuasively that he put one young woman completely under the spell of the music and of his own personality.

This woman was Mathilde Wesendonck, who had first come to Zürich with her rich silk-merchant husband Otto on October 21, 1850, in search of property to buy for a home. By April, 1851, they had settled in Zürich, where Mathilde took a lively interest in the intellectual and especially the musical life of the city. It was only natural that she should wish to meet Richard Wagner, the one celebrity of the place and a man whose name was now famous.

Mathilde and Richard first met at the home of a general, probably soon after the Wesendoncks' arrival in Zürich in the fall of 1850. By the following year, the Wesendoncks and the Wagners had become friends. After the Beethoven concert in 1852, the sympathy between the idealistic, pretty, intelligent Mathilde Wesendonck and the aspiring, sensitive composer ripened into spiritual intimacy. Although their friendship remained platonic, it represented that identity of two souls usually associated with a passionate love affair.

Mathilde's tastes had not been corrupted by a fondness for the kind of opera that Wagner was fighting to revolutionize. She was, as she herself later wrote, "a blank white page." Wagner quickly began, as it were, writing his own ideas and ideals on that page. He found the paper perfect for his pen. Since he had an insatiable desire to teach and convert others, he was thrilled to have such a responsive disciple as Mathilde Wesendonck.

Minna, however, grew less and less pleased with Mathilde Wesendonck. Minna had already begun to be troubled with heart disease. This, and the drugs she took for it, affected her attitudes and perhaps even her mind. She was no longer pretty and she had grown stout. Richard and she had again fallen "out of tune with each other," as he expressed the situation later. Still he needed Minna enough to be anxious and protective about her health.

Wagner himself had been in poor health, and had been taking drastic "water cures," then a new fad. They seemed only to make him more wretched, for they deprived him of the luxurious food and wine he craved and of the snuff he loved to take habitually. He again felt bitterly lonely, deprived of communication with persons who understood his aspirations, and neglected by the Zürichers. With typical egoism, Wagner could not understand why these worthy enough people were not wholly concerned with his deprivations. In turn, they resented his resentment.

The real cause of Wagner's physical and mental depression was his struggle to bring *The Ring* into being. The poems of the two dramas he had planned—*The Valkyrie* and *The Rhinegold*—were finished on July 1, 1852, and November 3, 1852, respectively. Wagner had read them to Mathilde Wesendonck, and she had found them, she said, "delightful." These new, preliminary dramas in the cycle had necessitated changes in "Young Siegfried" and "Siegfried's Death." The conversion of the two into *Siegfried* and *The Twilight of the Gods* had to be made before Wagner felt he could begin systematically composing the music for the tetralogy. The more Wagner contemplated this huge undertaking, the more overwhelming it seemed and the more external matters irritated him. He grew subject to violent fits of temper.

No other composer had ever faced such a task. Wagner did not want to write music that would merely fit the text of his four dramas. He saw that the whole tetralogy must be an organic musical unity. Each of the motifs he would use had to express its own emotional significance. They also had to be interrelated with one another so as to convey the psychological meaning of the work from the motif of the Rhine with which *The Rhinegold* opens all the way to the same motif which closes *The Twilight of the Gods.* These motifs also had to be constructed so that they could be played by the orchestra in counterpoint to the music a character might be singing. And they had to be capable of change according to the part each motif was called upon to play as the action of the drama changed.

To relieve the pressure of finding a means to execute these conceptions, Wagner took a mountain-climbing trip and another health "cure" in the summer of 1853. His return from it to Zürich meant only a return to his mental agony. He went away again, this time to Italy, in another search for release. There, in Spezia, on the night of September 3, as Wagner lay sick and exhausted on his hotel bed, the waters of the Rhine burst their confines within his mind and began to flow in endless melody.

> I fell into a kind of somnolent state [Wagner wrote in his autobiography] in which I suddenly felt as though I were sinking in swiftly flowing water. The rushing sound formed itself in my brain into a musical sound, the chord of E flat major, which continually reechoed in broken forms; these broken chords seemed to be melodic passages of increasing motion, yet the pure triad of E flat major never changed, but seemed by its continuance to impart infinite significance to the element in which I was sinking. I awoke in sudden terror from my doze, feeling as though the waves were rushing high above my head. I at once recognized that the orchestral overture to *The Rhinegold,* which must long have lain latent within me, though it had been unable to find definite form, had at last been revealed to me. I then quickly realized my own nature; the stream of life was not to flow to me from without, but from within. I decided to return to Zürich immediately, and begin the composition of my great poem.

Once free from the fearful tension of searching for a means of expression in music, Wagner forgot his ill health and his mood of depression. He worked with steadfast zeal at the music of *The Rhinegold* and *The*

Valkyrie. By the end of 1854 the basic scores of both had been completed.

The speed with which Wagner accomplished this work was partially due to the absence of the distracting Minna. In August, 1854, Minna, whose heart condition was growing worse, needed rest. She went to visit her relatives in Germany. In Dresden she worked hard to procure a pardon for Richard from the new king of Saxony, Johann, so that her husband might return to Germany to see to the production of his operas. In Berlin she labored to get *Tannhäuser* produced there.

During Minna's absence, Richard found the feminine companionship he needed in Mathilde Wesendonck. Her feelings for him, other than her intense interest in his work, are unknown. It is clear, however, that Richard was deeply in love with her and drew inspiration from her presence. The manuscript of *The Valkyrie* bears cryptic messages to Mathilde, ranging from the initials on the Prelude, which stand for "Blessed be Mathilde," to more explicit indications of Wagner's feelings, such as "I love you infinitely," "Do you love me, Mathilde?" and "Why have you left me, beloved?"

Since most of these coded records of Wagner's infatuation with Mathilde occur in the first act of *The Valkyrie,* it seems clear that the passionate love music Wagner was writing for Siegmund and his twin sister Sieglinde, the wife of Siegmund's host, was an expression of his feelings toward Otto Wesendonck's wife, Wagner's spiritual twin.

As he worked on the score of *The Valkyrie,* Wagner also seemed to conceive the music for the towering figure of Brünnhilde in terms of his growing understanding of what Mathilde Wesendonck meant to him. In the second act of that music drama, Brünnhilde executes the implicit wish that lies behind the explicit command of her father Wotan, the chief of the gods. She has seen into his mind and discerned his desires. She is Wotan's "wish child" who knows the secrets of her father's intentions, the only person the god truly loves. Wotan has to renounce this love by banishing Brünnhilde in order to maintain the moral order of the world.

In September and October of 1854, Wagner would come to the Wesendoncks' in the late afternoon to play for Mathilde what he had composed of *The Valkyrie* earlier in the day. Mathilde wrote of him:

> He called himself the "twilight man." Dreariness was unknown to him. He supplied the stimulus where it was needed. If he happened to come into the room obviously tired and strained, it was beautiful to see how after a short rest and some refreshment, his face would clear and a gleam light up his features as he seated himself at the piano.

Wagner was five feet, five and a half inches in height. His hair and his eyebrows were brown; his eyes blue and piercing. A visitor in 1854 remarked of Wagner's eyes: "Whoever has looked once into [them] will never again forget the deep and mysterious expression that shone there. There was something marvelous about his eyes."

Wagner's large nose had by this time become beak-like. His chin was round and so massive that it seemed to one observer to be carved out of stone. The same witness reports that Wagner had an unusually large head with a forehead that reminded him of an art museum. Everyone noticed Wagner's animated, dynamic manner.

Minna's daughter Nathalie, who did the housekeeping for the Wagners for some time in Zürich, later recalled that Wagner then wore "snow-white trousers; sky-blue tailcoat with large buttons, projecting cuffs; extremely high, black top-hat with narrow brim; a stick as high as himself with a huge gold knob; bright, saffron-yellow, glacé kid gloves."

Poor Nathalie was no favorite of Richard's. She was not good-looking and she was practically a moron. She and Minna, whom even then Nathalie still believed to be her sister, argued incessantly and drove Wagner frantic. Wagner was kind to his stepdaughter, but he never accepted her, as he did his pets, as a substitute for the children he did not yet have.

The intense creative effort that the orchestral music of *The Valkyrie* was costing Wagner put a tremendous drain on his emotional resources. So much of his energy was being poured into that music drama, which he knew would only half fulfill his total project of *The Ring* tetralogy, that he himself felt empty. He kept thinking pessimistically about the emptiness of all human effort. In addition, the hopelessness of the situation in regard to his feelings for Mathilde Wesendonck made him brood on the hopelessness of human existence.

The struggle to bring *The Ring* into existence and the frustration of his yearning to be joined with the spiritually sympathetic Mathilde led Wagner into a slavish and not very perceptive worship of the pessimistic thinking of the aged Frankfurt philosopher Arthur Schopenhauer. Schopenhauer reasoned that human desires, which are ultimately futile, cause all the pain in life. Contemplating works of art and listening to music can bring temporary relief from the pain of existence, but final redemption from this suffering comes only with renunciation of those desires.

Wagner convinced himself that this was what he himself had been thinking all the time. The music he was creating and was to create would be a boon to mankind. He also saw himself as the embodiment of Schopenhauer's theory of the tragedy of the human condition. He longed to escape into a timeless, spaceless—and quite imaginary—state of being, free from the limitations of human existence, which Oriental religion calls Nirvana. He even fooled himself into believing that he was practicing what Schopenhauer preached.

Such practice is, of course, impossible for a human being who is a time-space defined creature of flesh and blood and thus directed by the desires that spring from flesh and blood. All a mortal may do is control those desires by reasoning that survival requires the suppression or redirection of some of them. Wagner seems to have overlooked the fact that Schopenhauer made this limitation quite clear. Schopenhauer also emphasized that "there is no one philosophy existing or acceptable for everybody; the difference in degrees of intelligence is too great for that."

Wagner, however, immediately classified himself among those "men of genius" to which Schopenhauer claimed to belong and to whom he addressed himself. But by "men of genius" Schopenhauer meant intuitive thinkers. Wagner was not so much a thinker as a doer. He could no more cease to be driven by his desires than he could stop breathing—or stop preaching the theories of Schopenhauer to his often exasperated friends. Ironically, Wagner's study of Schopenhauer made him even more willful and more subject to his personal desires than ever—just the opposite of what Schopenhauer hoped his readers might become.

Wagner wrote in his autobiography that, as a result of studying Schopenhauer, "at last I could understand my Wotan." By this admission, Wagner seems to mean that he could feel in himself the tragedy of Wotan's necessary renunciation of desire. For Wotan is, like the gods that the ancient Greeks conceived, merely a projection of man himself as a superman endowed with superhuman power.

Wagner went on to say: "As usual with me, when hard at work at my music, I felt a longing to express myself in poetry. This must have been due to the serious mood created by Schopenhauer, which was trying to find ecstatic [that is, Nirvana-like] expression. It was some such mood that inspired the conception of a *Tristan and Isolde*."

In December, 1854, Wagner wrote to Liszt:

> I now take a delight in living for my wife. If love is to be measured according to sacrifices, no one was ever loved so much, since for no one have such heavy, deliberate sacrifices been made. . . . As I have never enjoyed the real happiness of love in my life, I now intend to erect a monument to this loveliest of all dreams, a work in which, from beginning to end, love shall for once be utterly satisfied. In my head I have evolved a *Tristan and Isolde*.

If Minna had read that letter, she might have wondered just what those "heavy, deliberate sacrifices" had been. She had returned to Zürich in November, 1854, bringing news that she had succeeded in her negotiations for a production of *Tannhäuser* in Berlin, but that Saxony was adamant about keeping Richard an exile unless he humbled himself by making a public apology for having been a revolutionist.

"I have become an outlaw for life," Wagner wrote to a friend, "an outlaw, an impossible person." Never, he thought, would he be able to supervise the production of his operas in Germany, much less ever see *Lohengrin*. By 1854, *Lohengrin* had begun to catch on in German theaters, and Wagner's previous operas, especially *Tannhäuser*, were being frequently given and in more and more new productions. But Wagner also felt "outlawed" from happy love through being tied, as he wrote, "by an impetuous marriage to a woman I respect but cannot feel to be mine." The contrast between Minna and Mathilde was now stronger than ever.

All this rationalization and self-pity on Wagner's part tends to conceal what was truly evolving in his head in respect to a *Tristan and Isolde*. He saw in the many versions of the story of those famous lovers that exist in medieval literature a projection of his own feelings toward Mathilde Wesendonck. In poetic fiction he could express and accomplish vicariously what could not be uttered or realized in real life. But Wagner did not even make a written draft of this transformation of his own feelings into a timeless story of love's consummation until August, 1857. In the intervening two and a half years, however, it could not have been out of his thoughts for long.

A season of conducting concerts in London during the first six months of 1855 disgusted Wagner with the materialism he found in England. The experience led him to an appreciation of the otherworldly idealism he found in Oriental religious literature. Through studying Buddha's life and his teaching that renunciation of desire is the key to bliss, Wagner found an escape from the disappointments of the London concerts. Wagner seriously considered creating a music drama on the life of Buddha, to be called "The Victors," symbolizing the triumph of the metaphysical world over the physical one.

Back in Zürich, Wagner worked at scoring the orchestration of *The Valkyrie,* which he finished on March 23, 1856. The emotional effect of depicting in music Wotan's sorrowful renunciation of Brünnhilde in the last scene of that work left Wagner exhausted. It seems, however, to have relieved him vicariously of the agony he foresaw in the necessity of ultimately renouncing his love for Mathilde Wesendonck, who he had come to believe was his inspiration.

Wagner's emotional conflicts brought on a return of his old skin disease, erysipelas, in the summer of 1856. After a rigid health cure, he began, on September 22, 1856, the music for *Siegfried,* the third music drama of *The Ring* tetralogy. The Wesendoncks left Zürich to spend the winter in Paris while their elegant new house, "Green Hill," was being built in a suburb of Zürich. Wagner perhaps felt released by Mathilde's absence. The first-act music of *Siegfried* emerged full of the joy of youth and hope.

That mood, however, did not possess Wagner long. In letters to the Wesendoncks he complained about the way he was being distracted by the noise of music makers and of a tinker who lived near his apartment on the Zeltweg in the heart of Zürich. Probably due to Mathilde's urging, Otto Wesendonck bought a cottage adjoining his own estate and assigned it to Wagner for a token rent. Previously he had lent Wagner money. Otto Wesendonck was wise enough to appreciate Mathilde's basic fidelity to him and their children, and to see that he could best keep her love by letting her sympathies wander. He understood them properly as being intellectual interests.

Richard and Minna moved into this blissful retreat at the end of April, 1857. The cottage had a beautiful view of the lake, and was surrounded by a charming garden. Wagner called the house "Asyl," meaning "refuge," though perhaps he named it that humorously, for the place had been intended as an asylum for the mentally disturbed. At any rate, he was overjoyed with it. He resolved never to move again.

The Wesendoncks moved into their palatial new home in July, 1857. Only a few steps away, Wagner was creating the music of the second act of *Siegfried.* The proximity of Mathilde, and her frequent visits to the Asyl, made Wagner's work unbearable for him. In the second act, Siegfried, the innocent child of nature, yields to the temptations of desire—for material power and for a woman. The story demanded that this desire be frustrated and that Siegfried be destroyed (in *The Twilight of the Gods*) by it. Wagner suddenly lost interest in *The Ring,* which had just been turned down by his publishers, Breitkopf and Härtel, and which the grand duke of Weimar was hesitating to produce, in spite of Liszt's persuasion, because of the cost and the difficulty of mounting the work.

Wagner had got to the music of the forest bird in Act Two of *Siegfried* when he wrote to Liszt, on June 28, 1857, that he had "torn Siegfried out of [his] heart." The statement is typical of Wagner's proneness to dramatize himself and everything he did. Actually, he finished the second act of *Siegfried* about two weeks later. The somewhat more sober truth of the matter was that Wagner could not keep out of his ears and his mind the music he was contemplating for *Tristan and Isolde*. "Today," he wrote in another letter, "Tristan intruded with a melodic thread which wove itself anew every time I tried to get away from it." This letter was written months before the poem of *Tristan* was begun, and years before the music was finished. Once planted in Wagner's mind, any impression or idea or experience grew like Jack's magic beanstalk.

Tristan and Isolde was clamoring to be written. In that drama, desire would not destroy the lovers. They would renounce the moral limitations of the world and find eternal bliss in a mystical union with each other through death.

The origin of *Tristan and Isolde* in Wagner's mind was that conception of ecstatic love. Mathilde Wesendonck was the catalyst, the precipitator, of *Tristan,* not the cause. In fact, Wagner later wrote to Mathilde in reference to *Tristan*: "My poetical conceptions have always been . . . far in advance of my experience."

Still, the parallels of the actual fiction with the reality are inescapable. Wagner-Tristan loved Mathilde-Isolde, who was the wife of another man, Otto Wesendonck-King Marke. Wesendonck-Marke was permitting the relationship by renouncing jealousy. In reality it was an insoluble conflict. In fiction, Wagner could solve it by imagining what he wanted to happen. He even invented the character of Tristan's squire Kurwenal, faithful unto death, for Wagner believed that every friend of his should be equally devoted and self-sacrificing.

Wagner brought his poem of *Tristan and Isolde* to Mathilde Wesendonck on September 18, 1857. The Prelude and the first-act music were finished by December 31, 1857.

The strain of such intense work was increased by the strain on Wagner's nerves of Otto Wesendonck's presence even in his own home. Wagner was fiercely irritated by the way that generous man seemed to be interfering with the accomplishment of Wagner's desires. Toward the end of 1857, Wagner exploded with rage against his tolerant benefactor. He fled to Paris. He had come to a decision, he wrote to Liszt, adding that every choice open to him was unbearably cruel. But, as usual, Wagner had no money, and so he had to go back to Zürich. The brief escape somewhat quieted him, and his return gave him an opportunity for one of the orgies of repentance and forgiveness in which he loved to indulge himself.

Wagner applied himself again to the music for *Tristan*. Minna could see no financial future for this work. Richard's dissertations on its philosophical meaning only perplexed her and increased her already strong suspicions that Mathilde's frequent conferences with Richard in his second-floor study at the Asyl, were not wholly confined to matters of poetry and music.

When Minna's total inability to comprehend her husband's psychology is taken into consideration, she can hardly be blamed. Actually Mathilde is more to be blamed for inconsiderately pressing her advantages of youth, beauty, intelligence, and wealth on a woman who was under obligation to the Wesendoncks. There was plenty of gossip in Zürich about Richard and Mathilde anyway, and Minna was not a secure enough person to be undisturbed by it.

By April 7, 1858, Wagner had made a fair copy of the music of Act One of *Tristan* for his publishers. The original, pencil manuscript of the Prelude he sent to Mathilde along with an eight-page letter—a "Morning Confession"—on that day. Minna took the package away from the servant who was to carry it over from the Asyl to Green Hill, and read the letter. She completely misunderstood that Wagner's passionate remarks were merely a commentary on a passage in Goethe's *Faust* that he had been discussing the night before at the Wesendoncks'. Read in that context, Wagner's words are no more incriminating than many other passages in his customary highly charged epistolary style.

After flaunting the letter at Mathilde, whom she apparently called an "arch she-devil," Minna succumbed to another heart attack. Wagner sent her away for a cure. Her absence did little to relieve the tension that her indiscretion had caused between the two households. When Minna returned on July 15 and renewed her tactless accusations, Richard decided that they must live separately. On August 17, 1858, Wagner left the Asyl forever, and began his wanderings again.

RW • CHAPTER FIVE

Shipwreck and Rescue

UNPLEASANT realities stimulated Richard Wagner's imagination to create fictitious situations which were more real to him than reality, and far more desirable. Consequently, the more violent the tempests Minna stirred up at the Asyl, the calmer Richard became. Her rages merely confirmed for him the rightness of the philosophy of *Tristan and Isolde*. Tolerantly, he saw her anger as the manifestation of a sick mind in a sick body. The dream world of *Tristan* was a healthy one. Wagner had to follow this dream. The illusion of *Tristan*, projected by his own misery, forced him out of the ironically named Asyl.

His new refuge was *Tristan* itself. The fact that the locality was Venice had little to do with the imaginary realm into which Wagner had escaped. He took a small apartment in the Palazzo Giustiniani on the Grand Canal, and redecorated it in a style that emphasized the illusion that he was quite shut off from the outer world. There he organized his working day, and became so immersed in the atmosphere of *Tristan* that he forgot his dependence on Mathilde Wesendonck for inspiration. He concluded that Mathilde had not been worthy of his devotion after all; she had not forsaken everything to follow him.

By March, 1859, Wagner had written the music of the second act of *Tristan and Isolde*. Then political complications regarding his exile made it advisable for him to leave Venice. He went back to Switzerland and settled for six months in Lucerne. In order to hush up the gossip over his departure from Zürich without Minna, he and the Wesendoncks exchanged visits. He was so desperately poor that he had to pawn the snuffbox the grand duke of Weimar had given him, and his watch, for he was supporting Minna, who had gone to her relatives in Dresden, as well as himself. His only income was an occasional fee from a new production of one of his operas.

Wagner's comfort was his absorption in *Tristan and Isolde*, in which he was expressing his own conflict between desire and morality. This conflict was being solved for Wagner by Tristan's fulfilling his desire and then satisfying morality by his death. The music Wagner was creating expressed passion expanding until it burst the bonds of time and space and soared into the timeless, spaceless world of love as an idea—the bliss of ecstasy.

The music of *Tristan* was finished by early August, 1859. Breitkopf and Härtel bought the publishing rights to it, and Otto Wesendonck generously bought the rights to *The Rhinegold* and *The Valkyrie*. Suddenly Wagner was fairly well provided for financially. He decided to return to the real world, where he might oversee the production of his works, and also hear some music other than his own. In September, 1859, he arrived in Paris, determined finally to capture that great musical center.

Wagner begged Minna to join him in Paris in the house he rented at 16 Rue Newton. In November, she arrived with the dog and the parrot. But soon they were quarreling again. Wagner repaired and redecorated the house at considerable cost, but a year later they had to evacuate it because it was to be demolished in the redesigning of Paris that was then in progress.

That reconstruction of the city, which was to provide it with the splendid broad avenues and plazas of today, had been planned to prevent any recurrence of the street fighting that the old, narrow, twisting streets made possible in the revolution of 1848. As a result of the revolution, Louis Napoleon, a nephew of the great emperor, had come into power. He wanted no similar revolution to dislodge him. On December 2, 1851, however, he had managed to overthrow the democratic government he headed, and to establish himself as Emperor Napoleon III.

Napoleon III's high-handed political maneuver had distressed the republican-minded Richard Wagner, and he had small opinion of "Napoleon the Little."

The Paris of this "Second Empire" was frivolous and corrupt. The government was much in the hands of a newly created nobility which, along with the diplomatic corps, exerted considerable influence on the vain, autocratic emperor. Wagner, therefore, was back in a political and social atmosphere similar to the one against which he had rebelled in Dresden over ten years earlier.

At first, Wagner's siege of Paris seemed again doomed to disaster. He was not only still a despised German, but he was an exiled one as well. Meyerbeer, who controlled the theaters because of the money his operas brought them, and the press because of the money his operas brought him, was now Wagner's enemy. But Wagner had letters of introduction to important personages in the Paris embassies of the various German states, who were also powerful figures at court. They saw to it that a concert hall was placed at his disposal; eventually they persuaded the emperor to allow Wagner the use of the Opéra. (This state theater was replaced by the present famous building begun in 1861.) The concerts Wagner gave were, however, a failure financially.

The high-born Princess Pauline Metternich, wife (and niece) of the Austrian ambassador, ruled Parisian society. Due to this position, to the importance of good diplomatic relations between France and Austria, and to her own charm, she had influence on Napoleon III. Partly to show her scorn of the newly created, conventional Paris aristocrats, and partly to champion one of her countrymen, the princess took up Wagner's cause. By the middle of March, 1860, she had induced the emperor to decree that *Tannhäuser* be produced at the state Opéra.

Wagner had hoped that his new *Tristan and Isolde* would be his first Paris opera. But a scheduled production of that work in Karlsruhe, in the Grand Duchy of Baden, had been canceled owing to the difficulty of the work, and the management of the Paris Opéra were, therefore, scared of tackling it. Furthermore, Wagner had conducted the Prelude to *Tristan* at one of his Paris concerts, only to find the Parisians baffled by it. They were accustomed to more purely melodic music, easy to understand and to remember, music in the old French and Italian styles which Wagner had abandoned. It has been said that with the third chord of the Prelude to *Tristan and Isolde,* modern music began.

What that facile statement really means is that *Tristan and Isolde* is the first work in the opera form to be written entirely in the impressionistic manner. Wagner intended the music to suggest rather than to inform. He designed it to stimulate listeners to contribute their own feelings as a result of the senses he excited in them. The audience was to become as emotionally involved in the atmosphere of the work as Wagner himself had been while he was creating it. Intellectual participation was not enough for him; his audiences were to be completely identified—first by feeling, then by thought—in the total experience of ecstatic love, not merely the particular experiences of the specific characters. Consequently, Wagner banished from the work any individual melody that might particularize a single character or a single emotion or a single situation.

In *Lohengrin* Wagner had first used this approach to involving the listener totally. In the Prelude to *Lohengrin* appears the same nondescriptive, suggestive music which Wagner felt was the only kind capable of communicating so abstract and mystical a conception as that of the Holy Grail. But the Prelude to *Lohengrin* is written in a direct—one might say, ordinary—kind of music. It does not have the oblique effect of the *Tristan* music. Moreover, *Lohengrin,* though advanced for its time, is still fundamentally a traditional opera with such set pieces as ensembles, choruses, and melodramatic contrasts. The music of *The Rhinegold* and *The Valkyrie,* which followed *Lohengrin* in order of composition, is closer to that of *Tristan and Isolde,* but the subjects of those two music dramas are not so abstract as that of *Tristan* and hence they required more musical delineation. The advanced music of the first two music dramas of *The Ring* had not yet been rendered in public by 1860.

Forced to lay aside his hopes for a Paris production of *Tristan and Isolde,* Wagner nevertheless determined that Paris must get at least a taste of his newer music than that of the fifteen-year-old *Tannhäuser,* which he had outgrown. Consequently he decided to write fresh music for the Venusberg scene that opens *Tannhäuser.* The decision was perhaps the most sensible maneuver of his career thus far.

Wagner's Venusberg music of late 1860 is impressionistic tone painting. Tone painting, which might be described as making pictures in music, was one of the innovations of the Romantic style of music. Hector Berlioz had laid down the principles in his *Symphonie Fantastique,* subtitled "Episodes in the Life of an Artist," which was first performed in 1830. In that work specific scenes are communicated to the listener by tones expressing the emotions that the scenes are calculated to arouse—a ball, a walk in the country, a march to the scaffold, a witches' sabbath. The whole is bound together by a musical scheme similar to the motifs that Wagner had developed. In his tone painting Berlioz put great stress on musical color, which he achieved by a wide use of instruments with different tones—from the harp and the flute to the trumpets and timpani—blended in an enormous orchestra.

Wagner seems to have reached the same objective rather independently, though, of course, he knew Berlioz and admired his work. In the 1860 Venusberg music, Wagner demonstrated his tone painting by creating an emotional atmosphere in which, under the influence of the sound, the listener may conjure up for himself all the delights of a supernatural world consecrated to the pleasures of the senses. Although these pleasures are expressed in the abstract terms of music, the listener can make them quite concrete for himself; he does not even have to look at the action on the stage.

The tone painting of the Venusberg scene is an extension of that of *The Rhinegold* and *The Valkyrie,* where definite scenes—the bottom of the Rhine, for example, or the smithies of the Nibelung dwarfs, or the rainbow bridge to Valhalla, or a storm, or tongues of fire—are rendered rather realistically in musical terms, while abstract ideas—hatred, fidelity, honor, duty, love, and remorse—are communicated by emotionally suggestive music.

Preparations for the elaborate Paris production of *Tannhäuser* lasted nearly six months. There were 164 rehearsals. These involved maddening delays, disagreements, bureaucratic obstacles, illnesses, temper tantrums, postponements, and every other hazard of theatrical endeavor. The management of the Opéra begged Wagner to write a ballet for the second act in order to make *Tannhäuser* conform to the pattern of the customary productions at the Opéra, but Wagner steadfastly refused on the grounds that it would be ridiculously irrelevant. He had written a ballet for the new Venusberg scene, and that was enough.

The reason for the management's entreaties was that the principal subscribers to the Opéra were the members of the socially powerful Jockey Club. These young aristocrats, who had no use for the pretensions of the emperor's court and its protégés, came to their boxes only to see the ballet, which was customarily introduced, whether appropriately or not, in the second act of an opera. The bloods of the Jockey Club were not interested in opera as art, or in ballet as a display of artistic dancing; they were, however, much interested in the ballerinas.

When the news reached the Jockey Club that the much publicized and eagerly anticipated *Tannhäuser* would contain no second-act ballet, the members resolved that on no account would they interrupt their leisurely dinner by getting to the premiere on March 13, 1861, in time for the first-act ballet, but would teach the upstart emperor and his upstart German composer a lesson by arriving at the Opéra at their usual time.

The first act of *Tannhäuser* went off well enough that night, and the Paris audience seemed to find that the opera, by now famous in Germany, was all that the reports had claimed for it. Then in the second act, shrill whistling broke out in the auditorium. "It's the Jockeys," exclaimed the manager with, as Wagner said, an air of complete resignation. "We are lost!"

The young gentlemen had come with a claque of whistle-equipped members ably directed by a trained leader. Instead of applauding, they roared with laughter. They shouted insults at Princess Pauline Metternich, whom they believed wholly responsible for this insult to their tastes and interests.

The rest of the audience tried to quiet the "Jockeys," but their efforts only caused a greater demonstration, and the result was pandemonium. The singers, however, went on bravely, not at all helped by the conductor, who was inept anyway, losing his place in the score. At the end of the opera, however, the enthusiastic music-lovers in the audience demanded many curtain calls.

The "Jockeys" repeated their hooliganism at the second performance five days later. By then, "Wagner whistles" were being hawked in the Paris streets by toy vendors. Not even the presence in the theater of the emperor and empress restrained the rowdies.

For the third performance, not a subscription one, the "Jockeys" bought up all unsold tickets and staged another demonstration. This time the exasperated tenor threw his big pilgrim's hat at them. Then Wagner withdrew the score, although several more performances of *Tannhäuser* had been scheduled.

Wagner's compensation for the three performances was 750 francs (about $150). The uncooperative and none too brilliant tenor got 54,000 francs.

Tannhäuser was by no means a complete fiasco in Paris. The production had been a splendid one, and the music had been much appreciated by those who had managed to hear it. The Paris press, embarrassed by the behavior of the young aristocrats, warmly praised the opera. Wagner may have lost the political battle, but he had won the musical war.

Eight months before the Paris premiere of *Tannhäuser* the king of Saxony had granted Wagner permission to enter Germany, but not Saxony, in order to produce his own works. Wagner's friends in the German embassies in Paris, and the rulers of several German states, had agitated for this qualified pardon. Possibly King Johann had finally been shamed into granting it by Emperor Napoleon's order that *Tannhäuser* be produced.

Free now to travel again in his native land, Wagner visited Karlsruhe in April, 1861, to reopen the question of a production of *Tristan and Isolde* there. The previous preparations for *Tristan* in Karlsruhe had made it clear to everyone connected with the production that only singers of remarkable ability could perform it. The chromatic style of the music, the necessity of the singers dominating a huge orchestra often playing at top volume, the unusually long and uninterrupted vocal passages, and the profound psychology of the major characters, demanded a training in rendition and interpretation that only Wagner could give. One of the reasons for the cancellation of the production scheduled for 1859 was that Wagner was then still banned from Germany. Now the grand duke of Baden authorized Wagner to procure and train singers for a performance in Karlsruhe on the duke's birthday in September.

On a return visit to Karlsruhe three weeks later, Wagner attended a rehearsal of *Lohengrin* for the first performance of that work he had seen. He was so moved by it that he was angry at having his mood disturbed by the introduction of Eduard Hanslick, the powerful music critic of the Vienna press. Wagner was curt to Hanslick, thus starting a feud that was to affect Wagner's fortunes in Vienna adversely.

With the exception of the Prelude, *Lohengrin* is an inferior opera. It has remained popular, and is still in the repertory of most opera companies, largely because its fantasy is the wish-fulfillment of many a young girl—her dream of a knight in shining armor rescuing her from a sordid fate. But the two principal characters, Lohengrin and Elsa, are insipid, and so is the music for them. Wagner intended Elsa as a tragic woman whose human need for love loses her the inhumanly noble Lohengrin, who cannot understand her humanity. Unfortunately, however, Elsa turns out to be a gullible moron, and Lohengrin a stuffed shirt. The interest is in the considerably stronger "villains," Telramund and Ortrud, the latter of whom is one of Wagner's most compelling woman characters.

The famous Wedding March, to the strains of which millions of brides have journeyed to the altar, is practically the only variation in the monotonous rhythm of the score of *Lohengrin*. And the continuous paging of "*El*sa of Bra*bant*" makes the stately setting of the opera distractingly similar to the lobby of a large commercial hotel.

While Wagner was in Vienna recruiting singers for *Tristan,* it occurred to him that since most of the possible singers were attached to the Vienna Opera anyway, Vienna was a more logical place than Karlsruhe for *Tristan and Isolde* to be premiered. The grand duke of Baden freely relinquished his option on the work.

Vienna had welcomed Wagner, and had produced both *Lohengrin* and *The Flying Dutchman* in honor of his presence in that great musical capital which had nurtured Gluck, Mozart, Beethoven, and Schubert before him, and was now the home of Johann Strauss, whom Wagner admired and who had done much to promote Wagner's music in Vienna. However, the usual problems in connection with preparing a new opera, especially so difficult a one as *Tristan,* arose. The press, led by the insulted Eduard Hanslick, said the work was unsingable. The opera management became diffident. Wagner saw that he could not hope for a production of *Tristan* in Vienna in 1861.

In October of that year, Wagner, who had gone to visit Liszt in Weimar, returned to Vienna via Nuremberg. He spent the night there and, on the following day, saw "some of the sights of the town," as he reports in his autobiography. The experience apparently revived in his memory the sketch he had made in 1845 for an opera about the medieval mastersingers of Nuremberg.

In November, 1861, Wagner visited the Wesendoncks, who were holidaying in Venice. He had also visited them earlier that year on their invitation. There was no hostility between them; both Otto and Mathilde were too sophisticated to have let Minna's misunderstandings at the Asyl shatter a friendship. Wagner, however, recognized that a renewal of his intimacy with Mathilde would interfere with her freedom.

During that visit, Wagner discussed the sketch of *The Mastersingers* with Mathilde Wesendonck. She seems to have encouraged him to proceed with it. On the train journey from Venice to Vienna, Wagner wrote in his autobiography, "the music of *The Mastersingers* first dawned on my mind, in which I still retained the libretto as I had originally conceived it."

The project of a new opera got Wagner an advance from Franz Schott, a music publisher of Mainz. Not wishing to spend all these new funds in an expensive hotel in Vienna, Wagner went to Paris, where he expected to be a guest of Prince and Princess Metternich. He found, however, that they had—perhaps deliberately—other plans for the use of their guest suite. None of Wagner's other friends in Paris was willing to risk harboring him. Consequently he had to go to a cheap, shabby hotel on the Quai Voltaire, on the Left Bank of the Seine, and there he began the libretto of *The*

Mastersingers in late December, 1861. He finished it on January 25, 1862.

Nuremburg may have revived the idea of *The Mastersingers* in Wagner's mind, but his visit to the Wesendoncks in Venice almost certainly influenced his rendition of the 1845 sketch of that work into a dramatic poem. In *Tristan and Isolde,* Wagner had worked out his passion for Mathilde Wesendonck, and the moral problems it entailed. Now he needed to express the nobility of his renunciation of Mathilde for, as he saw it, her own good. He conceived the Hans Sachs of *The Mastersingers,* therefore, as a noble figure who saw the madness of desire interfering with the perfection of art, and chose to follow the latter. Thus Hans Sachs, by releasing Eva to her true love Walther, becomes the mentor of both young people as well as the triumphant champion of the social value of art. By abandoning a futile pursuit, Hans Sachs makes a permanent monument for himself.

In that solution, Wagner saw his own future as a teacher, a force in civilization, and, above all, a free man liberated from passion's chains. Hence, *The Mastersingers* emerged as a true comedy, for the essence of that dramatic form is the triumph of a human being over his human weaknesses and the conspiracies of lesser mortals. Hans Sachs wins by losing.

Wagner wrote the poem of *The Mastersingers* in the same doggerel verse that the Hans Sachs of history and his contemporary mastersingers had used. An example of this, in Ernest Newman's translation, is Hans Sachs' pronouncement of the theme of the work at the very end of the music drama:

> if foreign kings should rule our land,
> no prince his folk will understand,
> and foreign mists before us rise
> to dupe and blind our German eyes;
> the good and true were lost for aye
> if German art we should betray.
> So heed my words:
> honor your German masters
> if you'd forefend disasters!
> Let us but take them to our heart,
> though should depart
> the might of holy Rome,
> no harm shall come
> to holy German art!

In many other respects Wagner was faithful to history. Hence, *The Mastersingers* exhibits another aspect of true comedy, the satire implicit in any exact rendering of life. Wagner seems to have conceived the sketch of 1845 as a kind of parody of *Tannhäuser,* also of 1845. Tannhäuser and his medieval associates were aristocratic poets guided by a high ideal in subject matter. The mastersingers were middle-class poets, tradesmen and craftsmen of a sixteenth-century city. Their ideal was a rigid form which often interfered with freedom of expression. Wagner saw them as pretentious fumblers, even though they were actually better poets than he makes them out to be. Indeed, much of the humor of *The Mastersingers* lies in the conflicts between their artificial rigidity and imitation and natural conduct and imagination. By permitting nature to take its course, the unpretentious Hans Sachs, the only real poet among Wagner's mastersingers, not only frees the young lovers from artificial restrictions but points out the social and artistic principle that however necessary and useful rules are, an imaginative person can rise above them and thus become a free, truly moral, and constructive member of society.

The poem of *The Mastersingers* was published by Schott in December, 1862. Almost immediately it became extremely popular because of its lusty humor, its fully developed characters, its realistic interpretation of the German character and way of life, and also because of the high quality of Wagner's verse. For nearly a century it has been regarded as a classic of German literature, and as such has been required reading in German schools.

Composing the music for *The Mastersingers* was far more of a struggle for Wagner than creating the libretto had been. By April, 1862, only the Prelude had been finished. Then complications in Wagner's personal life made it impossible for him to continue his work on the score. It was not completed until October 24, 1867.

In February, 1862, Wagner had settled in a small

apartment in Biebrich, a little town on the Rhine opposite Mainz. There he thought he would have the isolation he always needed while in the throes of composition. It would also put him near his friends in Karlsruhe and his latest benefactor, Franz Schott, who was soon to learn that benevolence to Richard Wagner could turn into a lifetime career of philanthropy.

Wagner sent for the furniture he had stored in Paris a year before, including the grand piano that Mme. Erard, the widow of the famous piano manufacturer, had given him in 1857. That piano had already traveled over a considerable portion of western Europe—an itinerary that makes amusing reading in Wagner's autobiography for anyone who has had to move a grand piano in these present days of easy transportation.

Minna and Richard had parted in Paris in April, 1861, more or less on the understanding that when he could set up a reasonably permanent home again, she would rejoin him. For the past year, Minna had been living with her relatives in Dresden. On February 14, 1862, Richard had written her there, perhaps unwisely giving her a choice as to whether or not she should come to Biebrich. Minna ignored the logic of the letter and saw only that the husband whom she had no wish to abandon was lonely and needed her. By February 22, she had arrived, after a twenty-hour coach journey, in Richard's refuge.

On the next morning a belated Christmas present arrived from Mathilde Wesendonck, whom Wagner had just informed of his new address. Minna remarked, as she herself wrote to Nathalie: "Well, that is certainly a peculiar coincidence!" Then, wrote Minna, "Richard started talking himself into a really savage fury." On March 4, Wagner wrote a friend that he had been through "ten days of hell."

By March 6, Minna was back in Dresden again. Richard had at last recognized that he could not live with her. He made no effort to divorce her, and faithfully sent her a yearly allowance adequate to maintain her. In November, 1862, they met in Dresden for a few days. Minna saw to it that they were so taken up with visits to friends whom Richard had not seen since his flight in 1849 that the couple had little time alone together. Wagner had been granted the right of re-entry into Saxony on the previous March 28.

After their parting Wagner went on to Vienna, arriving on November 15, in order to renew preparations for *Tristan and Isolde* there. He and Hanslick had been reconciled, and so the opera management dared proceed with the work; indeed, the management had requested Wagner to come. Soon after his arrival, however, Wagner, who had small use for critics, read the poem of *The Mastersingers* at a party where Hanslick was present. Hanslick immediately recognized Wagner's caricature of him in the buffoon figure then called Hans Lick but subsequently renamed Beckmesser. The battle between them was on again.

Quickly Wagner saw that the opera people were not

playing straight with him regarding the production of *Tristan*. Hanslick had unleashed his mischief again.

Throughout 1863 and 1864, Wagner conducted many concerts in Vienna, Prague, St. Petersburg (now Leningrad, USSR), and Budapest in order to support himself. He performed much of his own music, including parts of the still incomplete *Mastersingers*, and selections from the yet unperformed *Tristan and Isolde, The Rhinegold,* and *The Valkyrie*. The audiences were wildly enthusiastic. Wagner became the darling of musical Vienna.

At this time, and well into the 1870's, Richard Wagner was regarded as the greatest conductor alive. What his style of conducting was like is indicated in the essay he wrote in 1869 on the art of conducting. In this analysis he emphasized the necessity of a flexible tempo. His conducting featured a slowing down and a speeding up—a rise and fall—and he used *ritards* (gradual diminishing of speed) to connect contrasting passages. He based his beat on the phrase of the music, not on the bar line. For these innovations, Wagner was considered an anarchist by conservative conductors and critics, but his style influenced a whole generation of conductors.

Today's taste would probably consider Wagner's style of conducting too free and romantic. Undoubtedly it was a completely subjective interpretation of the music—better labeled (as Hanslick acidly remarked) "not Beethoven," but "freely adapted from

Beethoven." Certainly the performances would have been stamped with Wagner's vigorous personality. But Wagner had impeccable taste in music, and because of that probably did not distort any composer's intentions.

By May, 1863, Wagner had given up his apartment in Biebrich and had rented an expensive apartment in Penzing, a suburb of Vienna. He employed a couple to serve him, and he squandered the receipts of his concerts—and more, much more—on lavish furnishings and an excellent cellar of wines. On Christmas Eve, 1863, he gave a party at which the guests received sumptuous presents, which he described in his autobiography as "appropriate trifles." He added that he had "very little money, but solid hopes."

By early 1864, Wagner had to go to moneylenders; Schott had refused to advance him more money on *The Mastersingers,* which was already nearly two years overdue to the publisher. The prospect for another successful concert series in St. Petersburg collapsed. Wagner's plan to marry a rich widow who promised to take care of him fell through. By March, the demands of Wagner's creditors, who could have had him imprisoned, left him no alternative but flight from Vienna. On March 23, 1864, he hastened to the home of the wealthy Eliza Wille, whom he had known in Zürich and who was almost the only one of his friends who offered him any protection.

There, in Mariafeld, near Zürich, Wagner bewailed

the fate that had made him a wanderer and an outcast again. "The world ought to give me what I need," he shouted. "I cannot live in a wretched organist's post like . . . Bach. Is it an unheard-of demand if I hold that the little luxury I like is my due? I, who am procuring enjoyment to the world and to thousands?"

Eliza Wille's attempts to soothe the bitterly disappointed Richard Wagner came to an abrupt end with the return of her husband to their small estate on the Lake of Zürich. On April 29, Wagner left Mariafeld hurriedly for Stuttgart, where he hoped to arrange a production of one of his operas through the conductor, his friend Karl Eckert. He did not have a penny in his pocket.

On Monday evening, May 2, Wagner was informed at Eckert's home, and later at his own hotel, that a "Secretary to the king of Bavaria" urgently wished to see him. Wagner thought it must be one of his creditors in disguise, and only reluctantly agreed to see the gentleman on the following morning. Then Herr Cabinet Secretary Franz von Pfistermeister handed Wagner a photograph of King Ludwig II, who had ascended the throne less than two months before, and a ring. The king wished to see the composer at once, and promised him a production of *The Ring.*

If nothing else could have induced Wagner to follow Pfistermeister, that assurance did. The king had read Wagner's preface to the poem of *The Ring,* which was published in 1863. In that preface Wagner had outlined his plan for a production of his tetralogy as a religious festival in a new type of theater, with a new kind of orchestra hidden from the audience's view, with the right kind of singers, scenery, and stage machinery and technicians, and before a religiously conditioned audience. Only a German ruler with a true sense of duty toward German art could effect those plans. "Will this Prince be found?" Wagner asked at the end of the preface.

Ludwig II had already decided that Wagner's rhetorical question was answered. He himself would "give the impetus to a genuinely German style of musico-dramatic production of which," Wagner's preface stated, "there is not the slightest trace at present."

On the afternoon of May 3, Wagner paid his hotel bill with a snuffbox, got a friend to buy him a railway ticket, and just made the train that was to carry him to Munich and the king.

His "poor love-lacking life," as he wrote Ludwig II, had again been saved by luck. "That life," Wagner added, "its last poetry, its last tones, belong henceforth to you, my gracious young king. Dispose of them as your own property."

RW • CHAPTER SIX

Fortunes of a Favorite

LUDWIG II grew up in the imitation-medieval castle of Hohenschwangau beside a sparkling lake in the Bavarian Alps southwest of Munich. His father, Maximilian II, had had that rather hideous edifice decorated with murals depicting scenes from the lore of the Middle Ages, among which, in the Hall of the Knights of the Swan, was a highly romantic and artistically terrible representation of "The Departure of Lohengrin." In the rose garden of the castle a water-spouting cast-iron swan perpetually struggled to soar from the shallow basin of water encircling it. On the wall behind Maximilian's bed was the swan chariot of Rinaldo and Armida, the lovers of Tasso's *Jerusalem Delivered.* And in the park of the castle was a model of the legendary Fortress of the Holy Grail as conceived by some unimaginative nineteenth-century architect.

One of the earliest portraits of the future king of Bavaria appears in a sentimental painting of him, his mother, and his younger brother feeding the swans in the royal park. Ludwig's favorite subject in his drawing lessons was a swan; at least one of these early efforts of his to express his fascination with swans has been preserved. Another portrait of Prince Ludwig at the age of five shows him beside a tower he has made of toy building-blocks. His passion for building was to cost him his throne and his life.

Perhaps the most influential experience of Ludwig's life was a performance of *Lohengrin* which he attended in Munich on February 2, 1861, when he was fifteen and a half years old. The world of the mystic knight in silver armor and his swan suddenly became far more real and desirable to the prince than the dreary existence he led under the tyranny of his strict father and his unimaginative Prussian mother. He read Wagner's prose works; he learned the texts of Wagner's dramas by heart; he commanded performances of *Lohengrin,* at each one of which he became more and more obsessed with the belief that he and the Knight of the Swan were one. The prose style of his letters began to resemble the alliterative verse of *The Rhinegold* and *The Valkyrie.* He sealed his letters with a cross and a swan. He had a Lohengrin costume made for himself, and when he went walking, tried to find "Lohengrin types" in the people he passed.

On March 10, 1864, the unexpected death of King Maximilian II brought his eighteen-and-a-half-year-old son to the throne of Bavaria. As Ludwig II followed the coffin of his father through the streets of Munich, the Bavarian people cheered their new ruler. They saw him as a fairy-tale prince, for he was extremely handsome, tall and straight and muscular, and his blue velvet cloak in the spring sunshine enhanced the poetic, dreamy expression of his dark eyes.

Ludwig II's first speech to his people was simple and direct. He promised them that he would be nothing less than God's representative to them, and would strive for the highest ideals in his private life.

The Bavarians were glad to hear that promise. The new king's grandfather, Ludwig I, had been deposed for squandering his people's money on the British adventuress Lola Montez, and was still living in exile in Nice. The adoring Bavarians did not know that their new king had promised himself to install Richard Wagner in his affections as soon as possible, or that they would soon experience another Lola Montez. For, on April 14, 1864, Ludwig sent Pfistermeister on a mission to find Richard Wagner and bring him to the king.

It seems clear that Ludwig II never outgrew his childhood fantasies, rather that they grew in his mind until they obscured realities. Whether or not Ludwig II was truly demented—he was later adjudged mentally incompetent, but on the diagnosis of only one doctor—he was certainly unconventional. He had a pathological hatred of crowds, ceremonies, and people in general—in fact, of everyone and everything that intruded into the world of illusion which was the only comforting one for him. In Richard Wagner he fully believed that he had found the only other living person who understood that world as well as he.

On the afternoon of May 4, 1864, the young, inexperienced king met his considerably older and more worldly-wise ideal for the first time. They spent an hour and a half alone in an interview that was probably as much a mystic experience for the one as for the other. Ludwig had found, as he wrote, "the sole source of my delight"; Wagner, as he wrote a friend, had found, "the ideal fulfillment of my desires"—and at a crucial moment in his career.

On the following day King Ludwig wrote to Wagner: "Rest assured that I will do everything in my power to make up to you for what you have suffered in the past. The mean cares of everyday life I will banish from you for ever; I will procure for you the peace you have longed for in order that you may be free to spread the mighty wings of your genius in the pure aether of rapturous art. . . ."

In return, Wagner was to be the idealistic young monarch's friend. His sole obligation to his new benefactor was to commune alone with the king whenever Ludwig needed spiritual companionship. The sovereign at once gave Wagner enough money to settle the most pressing of his debts in Vienna, granted him a yearly allowance, and installed him in a villa on the

Starnbergersee (Starnberg Lake) a short distance from Ludwig's country palace of Berg.

In mid-June, 1864, state business called Ludwig away from the beautiful countryside around the lake. Without the ecstatic diversion of expounding his philosophy and insinuating his plans to the king in their almost daily sessions alone together, Wagner grew lonely in his lakeside villa. He wrote to many of his friends in the musical world, insisting that they join him there, and flew into temper tantrums when they replied that they were busy elsewhere. But on June 29, 1864, Cosima von Bülow arrived with her two children.

Cosima von Bülow was the daughter of Franz Liszt. In 1857 she had married Hans von Bülow, who, after hearing *Lohengrin* in 1850, had forsaken the study of law to devote his life to music. He had studied conducting with Wagner in Zürich, and piano with Liszt in Weimar, and was a favorite pupil of both. He was a gifted musician, but of unstable personality, largely because of the interference in his life of his domineering mother. Cosima's marriage to Hans von Bülow was by no means a tranquil or happy one.

Wagner met Cosima for the first time in October, 1857. Thereafter the Bülows had frequently visited him. As early as 1858, Wagner and Cosima had felt attracted to each other. When they met in Biebrich in 1862, Cosima was already disappointed in Hans's failure to develop as a composer, owing to his feeling of inferiority to Wagner and Liszt. It was then that Wagner noticed in the expression of Cosima's eyes that he had replaced Hans von Bülow as her ideal of what her lover should be.

Cosima was much like her mother, a brilliant French noblewoman who wrote under the pen name of Daniel Stern. She had made Liszt miserable by seeing through his strengths to his weaknesses. As also the daughter of the even more brilliant Franz Liszt, Cosima could not endure the inadequacies she found in her husband, whom she had married out of pity and in the hope that she could transform his nervous temper into true artistic temperament.

Cosima was not pretty, but she was intelligent and ambitious. She was also stubborn and determined. She got her way by using her talent for diplomacy. She knew she could be happy only with a man of determination and of genius, even if he was old enough to be her father.

In November, 1863, Wagner visited the Bülows in Berlin. As usual he was broke; he had to sell a gold snuffbox for traveling expenses. Hans urged him to stay at his house, and hear him conduct a concert. On the afternoon of November 28, Richard and the twenty-six-year-old Cosima went for a drive while Hans was getting ready for his concert, which was to take place that evening.

"We gazed speechless into each other's eyes," Wagner wrote in his autobiography. "With tears and sobs we sealed our confession to belong to each other alone."

Thus relieved of their long pent-up feelings, Cosima and Richard attended Hans' concert, which they fully enjoyed, and went on to a riotous supper party. Richard spent the night in Hans von Bülow's house. The next morning he left after a pathetic parting from Cosima. She knew as well as he that a disaster had befallen them. They were hopelessly in love with each other.

Richard and Cosima had a week together in his villa on the Starnbergersee before Hans von Bülow arrived. The result was Wagner's conception of the *Siegfried Idyll,* a passionate symphonic poem based on themes from *Siegfried,* and Cosima's conception of a daughter, born the following April and named Isolde. The full *Siegfried Idyll,* however, did not see the light until Christmas Day, 1870.

It seems clear from the evidence of diaries and of letters that passed among them that Richard and Cosima informed Hans of their involvement with each other. Hans seems to have been, if not pleased by the situation, at least understanding and tolerant. Certainly he made no objection to taking the post of royal conductor and royal pianist which, in September, 1864, Wagner obtained for him from King Ludwig.

Wagner had found that after Cosima and Hans left his villa earlier that month, he could not live without Cosima. But his idea of bringing the Bülows to Munich was not entirely motivated by a desire to have Cosima near him. In Berlin, Hans von Bülow had been so overworked, and so harassed by reactionaries, that his frail health had collapsed. In Munich he could have a fresh start and a promising future. Furthermore, Wagner wanted him available for conducting Wagner's works. Wagner had great confidence in Bülow's abilities, especially in regard to Bülow's handling of Wagner's music.

On November 20, the Bülows arrived in Munich and settled into the house Wagner had procured for them. Cosima devoted herself to collaboration with Wagner in all his undertakings except, of course, the composition of his music dramas. She not only managed her own household well, but supervised Wagner's bachelor establishment and frequently entertained for him there.

A month earlier, Wagner had moved into the handsome, rent-free house that King Ludwig had procured for him—and later gave him—on Munich's most fashionable street, Number 31 Briennerstrasse. (This house was destroyed by World War II bombings.) There the monarch thought that his new favorite could have both the luxury and the leisure he needed to complete *The Ring*, which Wagner estimated could be finished in three years. It would be eight years, however, before that mighty work was done. Wagner decorated the house lavishly and expensively with the advance that the king, who was to own *The Ring*, paid him of 15,000 florins (approximately $6,000), with 15,000 more to come.

By November, plans for a production of *The Ring* as Wagner wished were being made. Ludwig decided to build for the festival a new theater to be designed by Gottfried Semper, the famous Dresden architect. Wagner produced *The Flying Dutchman* and *Tannhäuser* for the king, and *Tristan and Isolde* was scheduled for the spring of 1865. Wagner also laid plans for a music conservatory in Munich for the training of singers to render his music properly, and of conductors to direct his works as he had conceived them. On December 25, Hans von Bülow made his Munich debut as a pianist, and was well received by the public.

Not necessarily, however, by the politicians. They had already sensed the danger of Wagner's almost hypnotic influence over their young sovereign. The innovations that Wagner proposed and that Ludwig instantly approved they considered insulting to their own traditions. They wanted no repetition of Ludwig I's squandering of the taxpayers' money on a royal favorite, or even of Maximilian II's extravagant building operations. Lastly, they resented the appointment of the Prussian Hans von Bülow, who had already shown his scorn of Bavarians.

Knowing Wagner's power over the king, the leaders of the two rival political parties tried to enlist his support of their policies. Wagner, who had absolutely no interest in Bavarian politics, refused it. The politicians, therefore, saw him as not only dangerous and obnoxious, but useless to them as well. They began to induce the press first to ridicule him, then to denounce him as a traitor—anything to minimize his influence on the king.

In February, 1865, the conservative party won a round. Wagner had indiscreetly referred to King Ludwig II as *der Junge* ("the kid") in a private conference with Cabinet Secretary Pfistermeister. That bureaucrat lost no time in reporting it to his monarch. Ludwig, a stickler for royal dignity and etiquette, was so displeased that he refused to receive Wagner. The press made a great to-do over this incident and succeeded in dividing public opinion into those who believed Wagner was another Lola Montez, and those who maintained that so great an artist as Wagner should not be judged as if he were an ordinary mortal.

Wagner was so upset by the incident and the unfavorable publicity that he offered to leave not only Munich but Germany if his departure, so he wrote Ludwig, "can bring peace to my dear one." Ludwig yielded to the threat. "Remain here," he replied. "Everything will be as before. . . . Till death, your Ludwig."*

To that assurance, Wagner replied, "I live," and resumed his enthusiasm for establishing the music school and arranging the first performance of *Tristan*

* The reader of today should note that the extravagant language of the letters exchanged by Ludwig II and Wagner, and the terms of affection they used to each other, were quite customary in correspondence of that time in Germany, and are not to be taken absolutely literally.

and Isolde. Rehearsals for that began immediately after the arrival in Munich, on April 5, 1865, of Ludwig Schnorr von Carolsfeld and his wife Malvina, the only singers, Wagner had decided, who could properly fill the roles of Tristan and of Isolde.

The twenty-nine-year-old Schnorr seems to have been an incredibly fine singing-actor. His much older and quite corpulent wife was an equally fine singer, but somewhat more unsuited physically for the role of Isolde than the handsome Schnorr was for Tristan. Wagner had already coached them in interpreting his music, and thanks to his extraordinary skill in communicating his intentions, they had found the score far less difficult than it had been reported. They admitted, however, that it was taxing. (Malvina had not let her young husband strain his voice, perhaps irreparably, by singing Tristan in 1860.) Hans von Bülow was to conduct the performance.

The final dress rehearsal, on May 11, 1865, was attended by the king and some six hundred guests. Ludwig II honored the occasion by pardoning all the remaining revolutionaries of 1849. Then, on the morning of May 15, the day set for the first public performance, Malvina Schnorr became hoarse. All the distinguished men in music, and Wagner's friends and followers, who had come to Munich to hear *Tristan and Isolde* had to go home disappointed.

To Wagner's own disappointment was added the arrival of officers of the law, ready to arrest him if he did not settle an old debt at once. Cosima had to rush to the royal treasurer and squeeze the money out of him as another advance against Wagner's allowance. Also, as soon as the news of the necessary postponement of *Tristan* got about, wild rumors and gossip as to the cause spread through Munich. "I am fit for nothing more in this world," Wagner moaned to King Ludwig.

Eventually Malvina Schnorr recovered her voice, and the premiere of *Tristan and Isolde* took place on June 10, 1865. Although it was presented almost exactly as Wagner had conceived it eight years previously, and although he had achieved a great goal, he was depressed for days after the premiere. His mood was like the rueful melancholy that follows an outburst of love. Sadly he recognized that very few of the audience had come anywhere near understanding what he had created.

The principle reason for that lack of comprehension in June, 1865, and to some extent still, over one hundred years later, is that audiences cling too much to the text of *Tristan,* or to the stage action, which is minimal, and neglect to recognize that the music is the story. From the very origin of the Tristan story in medieval literature there had been overtones. That is the reason that the tale of the lovers was told again and again, each poet trying to say more of the unsayable than his predecessors. It was left for Wagner to express these unsayable elements of the legend in music.

Consequently, it is futile to attempt a description of

the music in words. If the existence of music in the world needs any justification, then that justification is the fact that music expresses what words cannot communicate—the essence of the universal emotions of mankind. This essence is, as it were, filmed over by the spatial limitations of words and, for that matter, of pictures. At best, words can only define a subject; they cannot convey, except by hints, its meaning. The meaning is the total communication between speaker and hearer, writer and reader, painter and spectator. When total communication through emotion is possible, then the unity of the communicators is possible.

This total communication, this union, is the theme of *Tristan and Isolde*. It is indicated best, perhaps, at the end of Act 2, Scene 2:

> ISOLDE. No more Isolde!
> TRISTAN. No more Tristan!
> BOTH. No more naming,
> No more parting . . .
> Both one mind.*

As that quotation indicates, "Both" express the theme together. If they spoke, the effect would be incomprehensible jargon. The music, however, is crystal clear. Here, as elsewhere throughout the music drama, the words themselves are only a concrete clue to the abstraction the music communicates.

* Translation by Stewart Robb.

That abstraction is the yearning of a human soul to be free from its solitary confinement in a human body. It is a longing to exist not in isolation but in union. It is the desire to escape from loneliness into identity—the at-one-ment that is the goal of much religious thinking. But this yearning is a feeling, not a fact. Most religions teach that man can only hope for heaven, and have faith in the existence of things not seen, and love the idea rather than the fact.

The music of *Tristan and Isolde* expresses this longing in the first measures of the Prelude. In the final measures of the music drama it is heard again. Wagner's intention seems to be that there is no ending to the yearning. Tristan and Isolde are merely symbols of it. The person who wishes to approach an understanding of *Tristan and Isolde* should try to let the music alone stimulate his emotions to the point that he hears the overtones of a story that no poet can express in words alone.

The words of *Tristan and Isolde* are few in number, a kind of verbal shorthand. The incidents on the stage also are few. Explanations are given only when the frustration of the characters' longing reminds them of the causes of their tragic fate. The words, the incidents, the explanations act as a frame for the music. They focus the emotions that the music expresses, much as the stage itself, or, for that matter, the opera house itself, does. Like a frame on a picture, they keep the attention of the spectator from straying. Most of the music drama could be rendered as a symphony and still be comprehensible to a sensitive listener.

The public of 1865 was not sufficiently educated in means of communication to appreciate Wagner's new method. They were prone to make the common error of mistaking the symbol for that which it symbolizes. They mistook, for example, the love drink of Act One for a magic brew. They failed—and even today most audiences fail—to understand that Tristan and Isolde had been bound together by love long before the curtain rises. They drink the potion in the belief that it is a poison which will spare them the misery of being separated from each other and will unite them through death and transfiguration. The most obtuse of the first audiences denounced Wagner for offering them a glorification of adultery.

Tristan and Isolde, however, did not have a chance to disturb such unimaginative audiences for long. On July 21, 1865, Ludwig Schnorr died after an illness of only a few days. It was some time before Wagner permitted another production of the music drama, for he would not have it ruined by inadequate performers.

Ludwig II had been so affected by *Tristan* that he redoubled his affection for Wagner. Since he wanted to know everything about the composer, he asked Wagner to write an autobiography. On July 17, 1865, Wagner began dictating *Mein Leben* ("My Life") to Cosima.

As a piece of prose, *My Life* is far more readable

than Wagner's theoretical or philosophical works, though it is, perhaps, more detailed than necessary. Since he was telling his own story at a time when he seemed secure for life, Wagner could look back with humor on some of the episodes of his poverty, his hair-breadth escapes from his creditors, and his feckless adventures. Sometimes the humor is unconscious, sometimes almost hilarious. Of course, there are other passages in which Wagner indulges in self-pity, and there are some, such as his mean remarks about Otto Wesendonck, that do him no credit. The record is not infallibly accurate; sometimes Wagner's memory was unreliable, and some events, such as the Jessie Laussot episode, he seems deliberately to have forgotten. On the whole, however, *My Life* deserves more readers than it gets nowadays.

The record ends with King Ludwig's summons to Wagner. Wagner had the autobiography privately printed in an edition of fifteen copies. The printer added at least one more copy, which he kept for himself. The work was not published until 1911.

As the summer of 1865 wore on, Wagner's feeling of permanent security began to fade. In late December, 1864, Gottfried Semper had come to Munich to discuss plans for the Festival Theater, and King Ludwig had commissioned him to build it. But Semper had got no contract, and Wagner had urged him not to ask for one. By September, 1865, Ludwig II was vacillating between the two plans Semper had submitted, and the king's cabinet was refusing to award Semper a contract. Those politicians were strongly supported by the businessmen of Munich who wanted industry brought to the city, not a theater, especially one so expensive as indicated in Semper's plans.

Another conflict with the bureaucrats arose when Wagner insisted that the management of the music conservatory he had founded be taken out of the ministry of culture and be made independent of government control. Then Wagner requested a settlement of approximately twenty thousand dollars, which was to be a kind of advance, in order to pay off more of his debts, many of which had been incurred by his extravagant decoration of the Briennerstrasse mansion. He also wanted it as the basis of personal capital which he intended to invest for future income. Since the king had no money of his own, he could only instruct the state treasurer to pay the sum to Wagner. That bureaucrat rather dutifully inquired what the "advance" was on, and recommended to the king that an allowance to Wagner be substituted.

Wagner now put into play all his extraordinary dramatic skill to convince the king that the bureaucrats were destroying him as an artist. Cosima also worked on Ludwig II's feelings by embroidering symbols of Wagner's operas on a cushion and presenting it to the king along with a flattering letter. Ludwig, who had been inclined to agree with the treasurer that Wagner would be better off with an increased allowance than with capital which might give him an independent income, surrendered to Wagner's and Cosima's appeals. He ordered the money paid.

The treasurer's revenge was to hand over the money in coin. Cosima went to collect it, and rather shamed the bureaucrats by herself carrying the heavy sacks out of the treasury into the two cabs she had hired to transport it to the Briennerstrasse.

The king's ministers were now convinced that Wagner had an evil influence on their sovereign. Their conviction was strengthened by the sly reports one of them kept sending back to Munich from Hohenschwangau, where, in November, 1865, Wagner and Cosima visited King Ludwig for a week. The politicians set a trap for Wagner, who by now had unwisely begun to interfere in politics. He had found that without getting involved in politics, he could not further his own aims, both personal and artistic.

Wagner blundered into the trap. When he discovered his error, he compounded it by losing his temper and publishing an article in which he made free use of the king's name and the king's interest in Wagner's ideas. He then proceeded to deceive the king by insisting that the article, which had been signed by initials standing for "Free Thought," had been written by Wagner's enemies.

Inexperienced and emotional as he was, Ludwig II was quite able to distinguish between Wagner the man and Wagner the artist. He was disappointed in the man and hurt by the deception, and so was susceptible to the exaggerations of the incident and the defamations of Wagner with which the ministers filled the royal ears. The cabinet insisted that revolution was imminent. Had Ludwig not compulsively kept himself so remote from his people, he might have seen that the man in the Munich street regarded the whole affair as ridiculous.

Ludwig II had no intention of being forced to leave his palace; it was far easier for Ludwig to ask Wagner to leave his. On December 6, one week after the indiscreet article had appeared, King Ludwig II exiled Richard Wagner from Bavaria—for six months.

If the king had known that his beloved friend swore never to return, he might have acted differently. When Ludwig learned what he himself had done, his personality began to disintegrate.

RW • CHAPTER SEVEN

The Masterpieces Are Unveiled

RICHARD Wagner left Munich at five forty-five in the morning of December 10, 1865, pale as a ghost and clearly in a fury over the way he had been treated. Much as Ludwig II had protested his undying affection for the artist, the fact was that Wagner was again an outcast and a wanderer. He had to leave behind his dreams of glory, his elegant house, and Cosima. At least, however, he had money in his pockets for once, and the king did not cut off his allowance.

Cosima returned from the railway station "in an indescribable state," says one of their friends, who added: "If he really loves at last—and Cosima seems to love *him* passionately—then I wish with all my heart that there may be a quiet happiness in store for both of them."

That wish was soon to come true. Wagner went first to Geneva, where he rented a country house with a fine view but in poor repair. Seeking a better place to settle, he moved on to the French Riviera. There a telegram reached him that Minna had died in Dresden on the morning of January 25, 1866. Wagner was free at last.

He returned to Geneva, where, on March 8, Cosima and one of her daughters joined him in the cold villa he had rented. He resumed dictating his autobiography to her, and by March 23, he also completed the music of the first act of *The Mastersingers.*

All through the previous winter, King Ludwig had written to Wagner imploring him to return to Munich as soon as the fracas there had blown over. The king protested that he would die if he were to be separated from Wagner much longer. Wagner relented enough to consent to return on three conditions: his allowance to be continued for life; the personal possession for life of the Briennerstrasse mansion; Bavarian citizenship. The king immediately granted the first two, but he encountered such opposition from his ministers on the third that he had to give up. He wrote Wagner that he would dismiss these hostile bureaucrats as soon as he could.

Wagner, however, found life in Switzerland with Cosima so peaceful and pleasant that he had no real desire to reencounter the intrigues and calumnies of Munich. Furthermore, he had come to see that, devoted as Ludwig II was to him, the king was neither intelligent nor profound enough truly to understand Wagner's ideas. Cosima and Richard found near Lucerne a fine big house named Triebschen, with grounds extending to the lakeside and superb views. Wagner asked Ludwig for an advance on his allowance in order to rent it, and the king sent him the money as a gift. There, on April 4, Wagner settled in for what were to be six peaceful, productive years, the longest time he had ever spent in one place. (The house is now a Wagner museum.)

Wagner urged Hans von Bülow to join him at Triebschen with his entire family, but Bülow was too occupied with his duties in Munich to do so. On May 12, 1866, however, Cosima returned from a visit to Hans, and settled there with all her children. Ten days later, King Ludwig II stole away from his country palace and arrived at Triebschen to celebrate Wagner's birthday. He offered to abdicate if only he could be reunited with his "dear one" and protect him from the world, "the thief of peace and quiet." Otherwise, the king said, he would sink into "despair and death."

Wagner sensibly advised Ludwig to be patient until the political horizon in Bavaria cleared, and to be less withdrawn from his people. Wagner did not want Ludwig near Triebschen, lest the king interfere with the arrangement that he and Cosima were enjoying. Ludwig II seems to have been the only person unaware of its true nature.

But Ludwig was not to be ignorant of it for long. When the Munich press learned where the king had been, especially at a time when war was imminent between Prussia and Austria—Bavaria was an ally of the latter nation—the newspapers screamed with rage against Wagner, Bülow, and Cosima. They published clear insinuations that Cosima and Richard were something more than just friends.

Hans von Bülow then came to Triebschen, perhaps to demand that Cosima choose between Wagner and him. He was so hypnotized by Wagner's personality, however, and by enthusiasm for *The Mastersingers*, which Wagner promised he could conduct at its premiere, that he probably did nothing to resolve the triangle. The *ménage à trois* went on tranquilly for over two months.

The Prussian-Austrian war of 1866 ended disastrously for Austria and Bavaria. Ludwig II was secure in the affections of his people, for he had, as Wagner advised him to do, visited the front and encouraged the troops. The defeat and humiliation of Bavaria, however, caused the fall of the ministry that had been so hostile to Wagner and the Bülows. Bülow, who had been forced to move to Basel, returned to Munich in April, 1867, and by way of apology for the insults he had suffered, was elevated into the king's service and given a decoration. It thus was highly advisable for Cosima to return to her husband's apartment in Munich, and she did so, bringing with her Eva, the daughter she had borne to Wagner on February 17, 1867, and whom they had named after the heroine of *The Mastersingers*.

Wagner finished the music of that work on June 22,

1867, and completed the scoring on October 24. The first performance was scheduled for the spring of 1868 in Munich. In order to prepare for that production, Wagner frequently stayed with the Bülows in the two rooms they kept in readiness for him. Singers had to be gathered from the major opera companies of Germany; new scenery had to be designed and executed for each of the four different settings; the crowd scenes required the participation of a choreographer. Most of the technicians were imported from the theaters of other cities where they had demonstrated their proficiency.

Wagner himself educated the singer-actors into the psychology of their roles, and trained them in every gesture. When visiting friends, Wagner frequently ignored the prerogatives of the master of the house, and he behaved in the same way toward the manager of the Munich Opera. Consequently, he scarcely endeared himself to that official, but he completely charmed the artists working with him. He was sure that the work would be a great success, and he was determined that the production should be flawless. The only difficulty in the six weeks of rehearsals was the fits of temperament of Hans von Bülow, the conductor, whose sickly disposition was not being improved by a long visit from his dictatorial mother, who cordially disliked Cosima.

For the premiere of *The Mastersingers* on June 21, 1868, King Ludwig II commanded Wagner to sit with him in the royal box at Munich's Court Theater. At the conclusion of the music drama, Ludwig insisted that Wagner acknowledge the tumultuous applause of the audience from the front of the royal box, not from the stage. These unprecedented departures from protocol offended the class-conscious burghers of Munich and plenty of others in the rigidly stratified society of Germany in general. But after the performance, the most brilliant that Munich had ever seen, even the newspapers that had been hostile to Wagner had to praise *The Mastersingers* as a work of national importance.

Under the leadership of Otto von Bismarck, the aggressive minister of King William I of Prussia, the peoples of Germany were rapidly becoming unified into a nation with a fast-growing national feeling and a sense that they had a religious obligation to extend German culture to lesser civilizations. The 350th anniversary of Martin Luther's defiance of the Church of Rome, and the consequent religious independence of many of the German states, was being celebrated throughout the awakening nation. *The Mastersingers* seemed a culmination of that celebration, for, like Martin Luther, Richard Wagner, through his music, had given the German people a strong, independent soul of their own.

The very first assertive measures of the Prelude to *The Mastersingers,* stately and stolid, express the joy and pride that the public-spirited Guild of Singers took in the art of poetry and in their splendid old city of Nuremberg. The Prelude proceeds with themes of glorious midsummer and romance and the exhilaration of inspired song and delightful touches of horseplay humor, to a massive conclusion that sums up all the pageantry of a people honoring dedicated fellow citizens. Then the curtain rises on the congregation of St. Catherine's Church singing a mighty chorale equal in evocative power to those expressions of the German Protestant spirit in the chorales of Johann Sebastian Bach and the hymns of Martin Luther himself.

The drama of *The Mastersingers* that then begins to unfold is, of course, motivated by love. It is not, however, passionate love, as in *Tristan and Isolde*. Rather it is a love that reaches beyond the individual object to a general objective. The particular devotion of the various lovers means less to them than their unselfish and obedient dedication to the principles of art.

By these principles Wagner symbolizes the bases of the good society. Self-interest, in the character of the fumbling, humorless Beckmesser, is the ludicrous element of the comedy. It leads Beckmesser into dishonesty and public humiliation. In contrast, his opposite, Hans Sachs, renounces his selfish interests, for he has the humor to see how inappropriate they are, how out of proportion to the circumstances, and how detrimental to the general good. At the end of the comedy, the people of Nuremberg shout: "Hail, Sachs! Nuremberg's darling Sachs!"

Hans Sachs therefore emerges as one of the great characters of literature. He is superior to all distractions from his purpose, even his personal wishes. His cobbler's trade and his poetic art, he philosophically realizes, are the only things that will guarantee his independence on the one hand, and his immortality on the other. Both are service pursuits; the one serves the physical needs of his fellow mortals, the other serves their spiritual needs.

Like all the great figures of comedy, Hans Sachs is actually a tragic one. A middle-aged widower, he longs for a home and a family, but he cannot bring himself to impose these desires on the young Eva, whose heart is pledged elsewhere. His nobility is his calm acceptance of disappointment. This poignant sorrow he turns into tenderness, and sees to it that Eva wins her young knight, Walther. Hans Sachs could so easily have let himself be Walther's successful rival—for Eva loves the cobbler too—that his generous freeing her of her sense of duty to him is deeply moving. He knows that only the free in heart are happy. He resigns himself to serenity; in the long run it will be more rewarding than the tumult of competition.

Hans Sachs expresses his philosophy in the heartbreaking beauty of the music of his monologue, in

Left: Ludwig Geyer, Richard Wagner's stepfather (possibly his father). A self-portrait. Right: Rosina Wagner Geyer, Richard Wagner's mother, by Ludwig Geyer.

Left: The earliest known (about 1834) portrait of Richard Wagner. Right: Minna Planer in 1836.

Richard and Minna Wagner's first lodgings in Paris, 1839 (now 31 Rue du Pont-Neuf).

Wagner in Paris, 1842, a pencil drawing by E. B. Kietz.

Otto Wesendonck.

The Asyl, Zurich.

Minna Wagner about 1857.

Mathilde Wesendonck.

Wagner at the time he was writing Tristan and Isolde.

Wagner's manuscript of the final music of Tristan.

King Ludwig II of Bavaria.

Cosima von Bülow and her father, Franz Liszt.

Cosima and Richard Wagner, 1872.

Richard Wagner and his son, Siegfried, 1880.

Wahnfried, Bayreuth.

Wagner's study in Wahnfried.

The last photograph of Wagner, 1882.

Death mask of Richard Wagner.

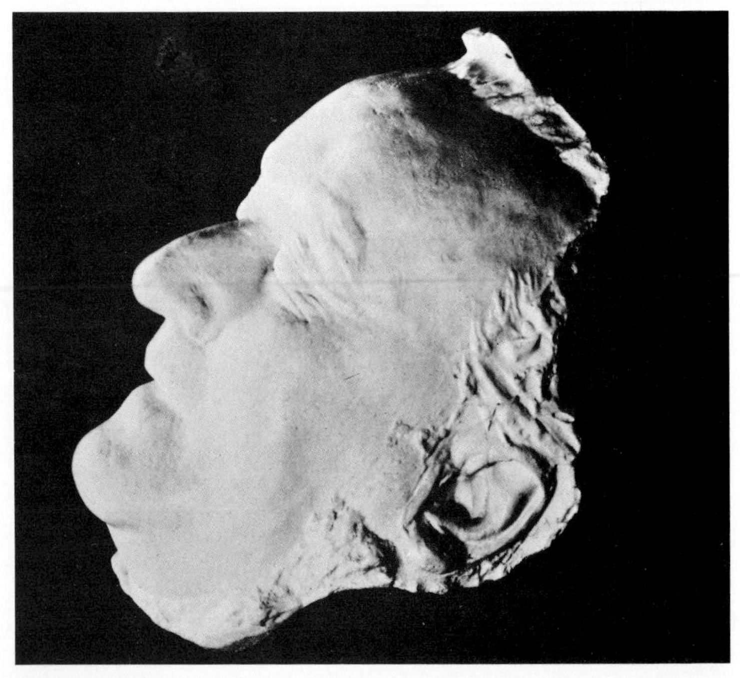

which he sings of the illusion that personal desire brings satisfaction. He sings:

> We'll see now how Hans Sachs intends
> turning this madness to his ends,
> that good may come of ill. . . .

The real drama of *The Mastersingers* is the conflicts in Hans Sach's rich personality—forceful and gentle, emotional but never sentimental, progressive yet treasuring what is good in the past.

Hans Sachs, however, is by no means the only well-developed or intricate character in *The Mastersingers'* list of sixteen personages more or less important to the action. Every one of these is characterized both by the words and the music, from the playful apprentice David to the stupidly malicious Beckmesser. Eva's father, Veit Pogner, the president of the Guild, for example, is a portrait drawn by Wagner with great love. In his address to the Mastersingers he sings:

> It oft has caused me sorrow
> to find throughout the nation
> the burgher stingy and mean . . .
> by lust for gold
> his mind controlled.
> Let us change that view and prove
> how much our art we love,
> that nobly, as man should,

we prize the fair and good.
This to our honor stands.

Pogner, like many of the other characters, is the very human symbol of a quality—pride in his calling and in his nation. Eva and Walther represent the essence of romantic youth. Nuremberg itself, no less a character in the comedy than any of its inhabitants, is the prototype of the happy community.

The Mastersingers calls for a vast number of people on stage at one time—the church scene, the riot scene, the multitude that gathers in the midsummer meadow on the river's bank for the contest of song. It is a gorgeous spectacle to watch. Its music is one continuous song in praise of music and poetry. Those who maintain that, all in all, *The Mastersingers of Nuremberg* is the greatest of all operas have plenty of evidence to support their claim.

The Church of St. Catherine is now in ruins. The statue of Hans Sachs in Nuremberg gazes at modern masonry. Only a few of the old high-gabled houses with their steep-pitched roofs line the banks of the Pegnitz River today. Still, anyone who has loved Wagner's *The Mastersingers* can easily recreate the "golden" Nuremberg of 1560, when the city was said to be the most magnificent of Europe and sheltered the painter Albrecht Dürer, the sculptors Peter Vischer and Adam Krafft, the humanist Willibald Pirkheimer, the explorer Martin Behaim, and the poet Hans Sachs.

After the triumph of *The Mastersingers*, Wagner tactfully left Munich. In the previous year he had had serious differences of opinion with King Ludwig. Although these had been patched up and the king had regarded the production of *The Mastersingers* as an achievement of their joint ideal, Wagner resolved never to have another of his works premiered in Munich. Quarrels between Wagner, his yes-men, and the theater director were one reason, but the principal one was a renewal of the gossip about Cosima and Wagner, and insults to her. Wagner and Ludwig II were not to meet again for eight years.

Wagner returned to Triebschen and began two more theoretical treatises. On November 16, 1868, Cosima and their two daughters joined him there. Cosima had decided to leave Hans von Bülow, who agreed to give her a divorce. Her action finally opened the eyes of King Ludwig, who was disgusted with her and furious at the deception she had practiced on him to get him to defend her. Ludwig saw to it that he would never have to meet Cosima again, but he and Wagner continued their fulsome correspondence.

At last Wagner had found the redeeming woman who would, like Senta in *The Flying Dutchman*, be faithful unto death. Cosima's diary reveals that she felt it her mission to live and die for Wagner. She protested that it was a "divine power" that compelled her to leave her husband, not that she wanted to or chose to. The opinion of the world, she confessed, meant nothing to her so long as she could "hold out [her] hand and say: 'I will follow you unto death.' "

On March 1, 1869, Wagner began the composition of the music for the third act of *Siegfried,* the music drama he had laid aside nearly twelve years before. This is the music that communicates the foreordained awakening of Brünnhilde from her long sleep on the fire-encircled rock by Siegfried, the greatest of heroes, who knows no fear, and the ecstatic consummation of the union of those two mighty beings. Wagner poured his own happiness into this music. It thus became an exuberant climax to a work, the earlier parts of which consist mostly of tedious wrangling and introduce Siegfried as an obstreperous adolescent.

Wagner had been at work on this final scene when he was awakened at four o'clock on the morning of June 6, 1869, by his housekeeper with the news that Cosima had given birth to a son and heir for Wagner. "He is so strong and handsome," Wagner wrote an old friend, "that I was able to call him 'Siegfried,' and in his honor too I completed my work."

Perhaps Wagner had made a mistake in enthusiastically writing to Ludwig II about his progress with *Siegfried,* the music of which he finished on June 14, 1869. It may have caused Ludwig to set his heart on a production of *The Rhinegold* in Munich, to be followed by *The Valkyrie,* and also a production of *Siegfried* as soon as Wagner had completed its orchestration. Wagner, of course, had intended *The Ring* to be produced, not part by part at intervals, but in a four-day cycle. Furthermore, having been elected, in May, 1869, to the Prussian Royal Academy of Arts, Wagner was thinking of Berlin, rather than "the hell" of Munich, as the birthplace of *The Ring*. He had changed his attitude toward Bismarck, and now wanted to tie himself to the tail of that statesman's soaring kite. Consequently, he objected, subtly but firmly, to the king of Bavaria's plans.

King Ludwig saw through Wagner's insincerities in the matter. Moreover, Ludwig owned the rights to the two music dramas in question; Otto Wesendonck had graciously surrendered them. There was nothing Wagner could do but fume and find fault.

Ludwig did his best to appease the composer. The best singers available were engaged and sent to Triebschen for coaching in their roles. The orchestra was increased in size. The stage of the Munich theater was remodeled in order to accommodate the intricate scenic effects that *The Rhinegold* demands, and Wagner was supplied with an excellent stage technician and a first-rate stage manager to direct in handling them.

Theatrical technique at that time was still rather primitive. True, gas had replaced candles for illumination, and the house lights were now lowered before the curtain rose. But literalness was the order of the day—Rhinemaidens "swimming"; Alberich literally transforming himself first into a dragon and then into a toad; a solid rainbow bridge from the gods' mountain-top to Valhalla. Such realism would make a modern audience break into titters of embarrassment; they would be too conditioned by the illusions made possible by motion pictures to be anything but depressed by mechanically animated dragons and nonluminous rainbows of paint and wood. Today Wagner's music dramas are staged with a very minimum of such effects, which are clearly suggested by the music anyway. Modern lighting effects also help the audience's imagination.

In rehearsals for the Munich production of *The Rhinegold* the sort of merry-go-round "horses" devised for the Rhinemaidens to "swim" on made the singers so seasick that their places had to be taken by ballet dancers, while the singers sang from the terra firma of the wings. The Valkyries were originally little boys (to give the illusion of distance) mounted on cardboard horses that were dragged along a raised track at the rear of the stage; later, an elaborate magic-lantern effect was fortunately substituted. Smoke powder was used for clouds, and Bengal lights for fire.

Difficulties with the scenery and the effects led to difficulties with the conductor and to difficulties with Wagner, who was sure that this production of *The Rhinegold* would ruin the work for all time. As usual, Wagner saw himself as the savior of art crucified by philistines. But the performance on September 22, 1869, was as well received by the public as any work so different from what they were accustomed to could have been.

The Rhinegold is performed without intermissions and lasts a good four hours. For a great deal of that time the stage is in semidarkness. The characters are not human beings, but gods, goddesses, spirits, giants, and dwarves. The only real touch of humanity is the giant Fafner's longing for a wife to keep house for him, which, in the circumstances is slightly comical. Wagner's use of recurring motifs to express such abstractions as hate, the renunciation of love, youth, or mischief is perplexing to anyone not familiar with the philosophy of the drama, not to mention the psychology of the characters. The music would have struck the ears of 1869 as senselessly deafening. In many passages it is almost patronizingly descriptive.

Familiarity with *The Rhinegold,* however, reveals its majesty and power. Even today the music is daring. It is a superb evocation of the moods of nature, from the rippling of the Rhine to the tempests of the mountains. The noble theme expressing the idea of Valhalla, the stronghold of the gods, is one of the world's greatest imaginative feats. The whole of the music, for that matter, suggests that the immortality of the gods is a reality. One hears the final notes with a sense that one has spent the past four hours in a timeless, elemental world, and has been refreshed rather than exhausted by being immersed in such imponderables.

The music of *The Rhinegold* glows with color. The

score of *The Rhinegold* calls for sixty-eight strings (violins, violas, cellos, double basses), three flutes and a piccolo, three oboes and an English horn, three clarinets and a bass clarinet, three bassoons, eight horns, three trumpets and a bass trumpet, three trombones and a bass trombone, one bass tuba, two harps, percussion (drums, cymbals, triangle), and eighteen tuned anvils (for the scene of the Nibelungs' smithy). Wagner selected tone colors from this array of instruments as a painter might dip his brushes into the various colors on his palette in order to give his forms an extra psychological dimension. For just as the color red excites the senses of the spectator in a different way from the color blue, so the tone of the flute has a different effect on his ear from that of the trombone.

Wagner used these tone colors for landscape and atmosphere, and also for characterization. Thus, the music of the waters of the Rhine begins in the double basses, and proceeds in the bassoons and the horns, as if the audience were rising from a dive to the dark bottom of the river up through the translucent currents of its middle level to the sunny ripples of the surface. The gleam of the Rhinegold itself is expressed by the shimmer of the violins, and its dazzling brightness, as it is fully revealed, by a clear horn and then by the trumpets. Valhalla is expressed by soft harmonies in trombones and tuba, with now and then a trumpet fanfare—rich, peaceful colors that convey the meaning of Wotan's supreme achievement, the gods' mastery of the world, and the just rule by which they will direct it.

Fasolt and Fafner, the giants who have built Valhalla, are painted in the somber, stolid, unsubtle, workmanlike tones of the trombones. On the other hand, Loge, the spirit of fire and craftiness and cynicism—not quite a god—is colored by violins, flutes, and piccolo.

In *The Rhinegold,* Wagner shows for the first time (in point of chronological composition) his mastery of the motif system he had introduced in *Lohengrin.* Early in *The Rhinegold,* Wagner announces the principal motifs plainly: nature, the waters of the Rhine, the Rhinegold itself, the ring, the renunciation of love, Valhalla, youth and beauty (Freia), etc.—some thirty-four basic ones. Then, as the action of the music drama becomes complicated and the interests of the characters conflict with one another, Wagner varies these motifs to show how the individual characters think of the subject the motif represents.

For example, as the crafty Loge describes the gold first as the toy it was to the innocent Rhinemaidens, the gold motif takes on a playful tone. Then, as Loge tells how the gold will confer power on anyone who will put it to use (by making a symbolic ring of it), the gold motif appears in the powerful tone color of horn and trumpet. And as Fricka, the goddess of women's rights, asks whether the ring could also be a feminine ornament, the gold motif becomes gracious and soft. Or, as the magic power of the Tarnhelm, the wishing cap, is demonstrated by Alberich's using it to transform himself into a column of vapor, the Tarnhelm motif is stated in the mystical tone color of muted horns. Later, as the abused Mime tells how he made the Tarnhelm which his brother Alberich steals from him, the motif is rendered by the plaintive bassoons.

The Rhinegold, of course, is only the prologue to the story of the effect that the curse of greed for gold has on the world and of how that curse can be removed. The impact of *The Rhinegold* on the musical world was so great that the unfolding of the rest of the cycle was eagerly anticipated.

If Wagner fretted and fumed and quarreled and felt despised and rejected over the intrigues in Munich in connection with the production of *The Rhinegold,* he also reveled in the sunny joy of his life at Triebschen. A brilliant and beautiful and charming young Frenchwoman, Judith Gautier, visited Richard and Cosima there in the summer of 1869, and wrote of the experience:

> The Master took us to a pavilion on higher ground, from which, he said, the view was glorious. The children were tumbling on the soft grass with little screams of happy laughter. . . . Richard Wagner stood upright, leaning both hands on the rough country fence, silent, and with the earnest expression of concentration peculiar to him at times of internal emotion. His eyes, blue as the lake and almost motionless, seemed to be sucking in the picture, from which a world of ideas came streaming to-

> ward him. This place of refuge, this delicious hiding-place, made secure for him by the tenderness of the woman he loved at a time when he was most cruelly pursued by the bitter things of life; this lovely shrine, enlivened by children's laughter, where the blows of fate could reach him only, as it were, over a rampart of love—it was of this that he was thinking with such thankfulness. . . .

Judith Gautier also told of Wagner's playfulness, possibly put on by him to impress her with his youth. He would push Cosima sky-high in a swing, climb trees, scale the side of the house by means of the mouldings and shutters. In the evenings he expounded *Siegfried* or retold the story of his life—and served excellent champagne. He and Cosima were living as if they were in a play; often, it seems, they deliberately dramatized their daily lives.

Judith Gautier also described the house itself: a drawing room with walls covered with yellow leather, embossed with gold arabesques; a gallery hung in violet velvet and tapestries depicting scenes from *The Ring;* statues of Wagner's heroes; portraits of Beethoven, Goethe, and Schiller; all sorts of rare and precious objects.

Another visitor that summer was Friedrich Nietzche, then a young professor at the University of Basel. His sister described Cosima walking by the lake in a pink cashmere gown trimmed with lace and carrying a big straw hat decorated with pink roses. Richard accompanied her in "a Flemish painter's costume—a black velvet coat, black satin knee breeches, black silk stockings . . . and a painter's beret on his head, which was covered with luxuriant brown hair."

Nietzche, also a genius, became fascinated with Wagner, and was greatly influenced by him. They became very close, for they shared the same hatred of the materialistic, industrial civilization of the mid-nineteenth century and the same worship of the civilization of ancient Greece. Nietzche, however, knew far more facts about the Periclean Athenians than Wagner did. The younger man was to become the most influential thinker of the new German nation, its very voice. His philosophical writings, his theory of the "over-man"—the man who "sublimates" his passions in creativity—and his denial of the value of confining morality owed a great deal to Wagner.

The two men later differed and fell out of friendship. Wagner rejected the militarism of the German Empire which Nietzche embraced. Wagner became more and more of a Christian, whereas Nietzche saw Christianity as too otherworldly and too repressive of human vitality to be an emancipating religion.

Nietzche suffered a complete mental collapse, and died when not quite fifty-six years old—Wagner's age when they met.

Also in the summer of 1869, Hans von Bülow began divorce proceedings. He wrote to Cosima: "You have preferred to devote your life . . . to one who is my superior, and, far from blaming you, I *approve* your action from every point of view and admit you are perfectly right. . . ." Bülow remained on friendly terms with both Cosima and Richard, and continued to introduce and interpret Wagner's music. But they never met again. Eventually Bülow remarried.

The divorce was granted on July 18, 1870. On August 25, Cosima and Richard were married in the Protestant church at Lucerne. Later Cosima left the Roman Catholic Church, in which she had been baptized, and became a Protestant.

In spite of Wagner's protests, Ludwig II had *The Valkyrie* produced in Munich on June 26, 1869. As in the case of *The Rhinegold* premiere, the eminent in the musical world flocked to hear it. Even the newspapers most hostile to Wagner praised it as a work of "gigantic talent."

Of all the parts of *The Ring, The Valkyrie* is the most human and therefore the most popular. The conflict is an elemental one—the force of love versus the forces of society. This conflict exists on a plane high above that of ordinary life, for all the characters except Hunding are either partly of a divine nature (Siegmund and Sieglinde) or are wholly divine. By making them divine, however, Wagner did not mean to say that they are spirits or prime movers or merely abstractions. They have some of that quality, and they have superhuman and perhaps magical powers, but they express their nature in wholly human ways.

Hence they enlarge the complexities of human emotions as if they were magnifying glasses held over fine print.

The "fine print" of the issues in *The Valkyrie* is Wagner's philosophy of the obligation implicit in love. Human relationships, Wagner indicates, are just as impossible without mutual obligations as they are impossible without love. The question Wagner raises in the scene that begins the action is whether an obligation without love need be honored. Is Sieglinde's desertion of her husband justified because there is no love in their relationship, and is Siegmund's violation of hospitality justified by his love for the unhappy Sieglinde? Is Fricka's insistence that Siegmund be punished justified by a moral law which, true enough, involves a love of order and propriety but has nothing to do with human feelings? Is that moral law, therefore, artificial and worthless? Is not love a higher, truer, and more valuable law?

The solution Wagner proposes for these problems is renunciation, a relinquishing of possessiveness. For the whole problem of *The Ring* hinges on who possesses the ring itself, the symbol of power over others. This lust for power, as Wotan acknowledges—and he himself has been guilty of it—will destroy the ideal world he hoped to create and maintain in serene balance.

Each of the characters fights to keep possession of what he believes is his right: Hunding for his wife;

Siegmund for Sieglinde; Wotan for absolute power; Brünnhilde for pride. Hence, no one is free, each being a slave to his desire to possess. But freedom, Wotan sees, is the only state in which the world order can exist. He contemptuously destroys Hunding, for example, for Hunding is a slave to Fricka's artificial morality; such a nature cannot benefit the world Wotan desires.

The greatness of Brünnhilde is that she understands this solution better even that Wotan. To achieve it she sacrifices her duty. Her identification with Wotan—"What am I, if not your will?"—leads her to disobey his actual command by obeying what he inwardly wishes her to do. What determines her is her recognition of the love Siegmund has for Sieglinde, which causes Siegmund to defy the doom that Brünnhilde announces to him. Siegmund's love has made him bold, a hero so great that Brünnhilde recognizes that she must obey her own duty, which Wotan has entrusted to her, namely, to free heroes from mortal limitations and bring them to immortal life in Valhalla. Otherwise the impulse to heroism would vanish from the world. Brünnhilde puts this duty ahead of her own survival because her obligation and her love are the same thing. Hers is the true heroism of self-sacrifice.

Renunciation without reward, however, is, in Wagner's thinking, no satisfactory solution. And renunciation without love—Fricka's demand—is even less satisfactory. The solution must, therefore, be to translate renunciation into forgiveness. Forgiveness is what Brünnhilde begs of Wotan, not punishment. Their love for each other has so identified them that Wotan recognizes the rightness of Brünnhilde's plea. Through this mutual love they reach a compromise. Each relinquishes a part of himself. Their reward is the salvation of the world order they both love, for their mutual forgiveness has made it possible for the hero Siegfried to redeem the world through his sacrifice.

The Valkyrie begins with music of a storm. It ends with music of peaceful sleep, as tender and touching as a lullaby. The meaning seems to be that unselfish love quiets the fearsomeness of selfish passions and brings serenity. No human voice intrudes on the effect of these two musical passages. The music alone communicates the cycle of emotions that Wagner wishes the audience to understand.

In between is music that conveys the human emotions involved in the complex problem Wagner states and resolves. The forces in conflict are so elemental in human life that the music which expresses them has tremendous affective power. It so arouses the emotions of the audience that they cannot help becoming identified with every one of the characters and sympathizing with them to the point of tears. It is fiercely dramatic music, but it is also exquisitely tender music. It is vividly pictorial music and also strongly suggestive.

Modern staging of *The Valkyrie* recognizes the power of the music alone to convey Wagner's intentions. Audiences no longer have to see the door of Hunding's hut blow open in order for them to understand that, as Siegmund sings, "Winter storms have waned in the winsome May." The lyrical strains with which Siegmund sings of his love make that change very clear. No lantern slides or merry-go-round machinery are necessary to help the audience imagine the Valkyries riding with rescued heroes across their saddlebows through stormy skies to cloud-wrapped Valhalla. Flickering orange ribbons are unnecessary to make the fire surrounding the sleeping Brünnhilde beautiful and terrifying; the flames are far more real when felt through Wagner's music.

The tenderness implicit in the relationships of the characters is expressed in music that is noble and full of infinite pathos. Brünnhilde's confession of identity with Wotan's will; her announcement to Siegmund of his imminent doom; Siegmund's comforting of the terrified Sieglinde; Wotan's vision of "the end," his contempt for Hunding, and his sorrowful leavetaking of his glorious, beloved daughter—all are stated in music so refined that no trace of effeminate sentimentality mars the dignity of those deep emotions. *The Valkyrie* is a drama packed with violent and often improbable action, but it becomes gentle and plausible because the music makes it felt rather than seen. It represents Wagner for the first time (1856) in complete control of all the elements of his new medium of expression—music drama.

RW • CHAPTER EIGHT

A Dream Comes True

ACCORDING to all reports and records of the productions of *The Rhinegold* and *The Valkyrie* in Munich, Wagner had nothing to be dissatisfied with in regard to their excellence. True, the stage machinery had not functioned perfectly, but it often does not even today. It had been a blow to his ego, however, to find that a first performance of one of his works could be adequately accomplished without his personal supervision of every detail.

The Festival Theater in Munich had been abandoned, largely because Wagner himself had lost interest in it. The music school there had become as conventional as any other. The political situation in Bavaria made it seem likely that King Ludwig II might be deposed. In that event, Wagner's allowance would probably vanish along with the protection that the king gave him against the Bavarian bureaucrats.

Wagner was, however, in a fairly secure financial position by this time, thanks to a steady income from theaters which were producing his works with constantly increasing frequency. Moreover, legislation was in progress which would soon bring him royalties on those works instead of a flat fee for the right to produce them.

At any rate, Wagner was determined to bypass Munich insofar as the future of *The Ring* was concerned. He must have a theater for it completely under his control. On March 5, 1870, Wagner's concentration on that problem caused a memory of a town called Bayreuth to leap into the front of his conscious mind. That evening he asked Cosima to look up an encyclopedia article on the town. Thereafter they would honor the date as "the birthday of Bayreuth."

The literal Bayreuth had been born in 1194. It was a provincial Bavarian town on the Roter Main River, forty miles northeast of Nuremberg. Its population was around twenty-nine thousand. Even today it is a little hard to reach. In the eighteenth century, a sister of Frederick the Great and her husband had made Bayreuth their home, and had beautified it with parks and gardens, rococo palaces, and a theater, the "Margravine's Opera House," finished in 1748 and still standing as a charming example of the rococo style at its height, had the largest stage of all the theaters of Germany even in 1870—all of eighteen feet high and thirty feet wide.

Wagner had visited Bayreuth in 1835. Probably, thirty-five years later, it was a memory of this extraordinary theater that revived Bayreuth in his mind. It seemed to him the very place for *The Ring*. By June, 1870, he had made up his mind on the subject.

On July 19, 1870, France declared war on Prussia in the hope of keeping that nation's dominance of European politics from spreading further. By September 1, the French had been crushed at Sedan, and Emperor Napoleon III was a prisoner of the Prussians. There followed a bitter siege of Paris during the winter of 1870–71 before terms of peace humiliating to France were accepted by the French on March 1, 1871. As a result, King William I of Prussia was proclaimed Emperor of Germany.

German national feeling rose to fever pitch after the Prussian victories. Wagner raised it even higher by a tasteless farce, *A Capitulation,* ridiculing the sufferings of Parisians during the siege, and by a vulgar *Kaiser March,* ending in a chorale of fatuous praise for Emperor William. As soon as peace had been declared, Wagner and Cosima left their refuge at Triebschen, primarily to investigate Bayreuth, but actually to make a triumphal tour of triumphant Germany. Wagner was hailed in Leipzig and Dresden, and in Berlin crowds gathered day after day outside his hotel just for a glimpse of the man who had made German music as supreme in the world as Bismarck had made German military might.

Wagner calculated that with all this frenzy of German nationalism, the time was right for him to launch his program for a German national theater. On April 28, 1871, he read a paper on *The Destiny of Opera* to the Royal Academy of Berlin. Berlin went wild with enthusiasm, hoping that Wagner would establish his national theater in that city. But on May 12, Wagner issued a pamphlet stating that he would locate it in Bayreuth in a theater built especially for his purposes. The Margravine's Opera House had, of course, proved on inspection to be too small and antiquated for *The Ring*.

Ludwig II received Wagner's announcement with extraordinary calm, considering the fact that he held the rights to performances of *The Ring*, and had already produced half of it in Munich. An explanation of Ludwig's acquiescence with Wagner's trickery is that the king had got bored with Wagner's petulant obstinacy. Ludwig had found a new world of illusion which he was proceeding to build out of bricks and mortar. He had already constructed the little palace of Linderhof, with its artificial grotto and lake in which he could play at being Lohengrin in a swan boat, and he had begun the fairy castle of Neuschwanstein on a mountaintop opposite Hohenschwangau. Ludwig seems to have willingly let Wagner outmaneuver him, which Wagner did by pretending that the score of *Siegfried* was still incomplete and so any continuation of the cycle in Munich would be impossible.

Another visit to Bayreuth demonstrated to Wagner that the town's bankers and businessmen were, and doubtless would continue to be, extremely cooperative with his plans. The national theater and the festivals of Wagner's music dramas would bring, they saw, enormous amounts of money to their little city, not to mention great prestige. By the end of January, 1872, the town council had bought land for the theater. It was now up to Wagner to find the money for building the theater, and financing the performances—an estimated $300,000.

One of the key points of Wagner's plan was that he was to be free from financial control by anyone else. He would head a committee of three, the other two members of which would be merely financial managers. The money for the theater was to be raised by subscriptions, for which tickets of admission to the entire cycle would be issued in exchange. An association of one thousand (later, thirteen hundred) patrons was to be organized, each of whom would buy at least one share at three hundred dollars, a sum that seems small today but which was a considerable investment in 1872.

Wagner's Berlin friends undertook to discover and organize patrons, and also to form Wagner clubs. The clubs were to be made up of persons who could not afford a share by themselves but could afford to contribute to the cost of one share or more that would be bought by the club, which would then distribute tickets to single performances among its members. There was to be no public sale of tickets.

In February, 1872, Wagner decided that he must leave his beloved Triebschen and resettle in Bayreuth in order better to manage the increasingly complicated work of realizing his dream. He bought three acres of land adjoining the palace park in Bayreuth for six thousand dollars and gave an architect instructions for a lavish house and luxuriant gardens. Then he rented a suite in a hotel near Bayreuth, where Cosima and the children, after closing up Triebschen, joined him in late April.

The cornerstone of the theater was laid in a driving rain on Wagner's birthday, May 22, 1872. The Bayreuth Council arranged an elaborate celebration in the old rococo theater as an advertisement of their town. To the throng of notables who had gathered for the event, Wagner explained that what was about to be achieved in Bayreuth was the realization of the thought of one individual and of those who loved and understood him.

There had been plenty of willing helpers in the fund raising, but by April, 1873, only two hundred of the thirteen hundred necessary subscriptions had been paid for. Wagner, therefore, undertook to raise money himself through conducting a series of concerts. Some of these brought in as much as eight thousand dollars apiece and led to the formation of more and more Wagner Clubs. All his herculean efforts in behalf of the festival, now scheduled for rehearsal in 1874, exhausted Wagner. He had also been working on the score of *The Twilight of the Gods* during the more leisurely summers. The exacting music of this last part of *The Ring* came from him with as much control as if he had had no other demands whatever upon his thinking. In the circumstances, this music is one of the most heroic achievements in art. But the drain on Wagner's seemingly endless resources led him to confess to Cosima that he believed his heart was damaged.

The "topping off" of the theater was celebrated on August 2, 1873. By then, however, only a third of the money needed for the project had been paid over. In desperation Wagner appealed for help to King Ludwig II. Possibly out of irritation over a misunderstanding, but more likely because he was wholly wrapped up in his own building schemes, the king refused. It began to look as if the empty shell would have to be boarded up and left, perhaps for ever, as a dreary monument to an unsupported ideal.

Refusing to acknowledge defeat, Wagner appealed for help through the grand duke of Baden to the emperor himself. This move seems to have changed King Ludwig's mind; he could not bear the thought of any other prince than himself being the savior of German art. Before Wagner received the grand duke's refusal, he got an apologetic letter from Ludwig promising a loan of $100,000. As so often before, Wagner had been saved in the eleventh hour of his distress.

A contract guaranteeing that loan was signed on February 26, 1874. On April 28, Wagner took possession of his new house, and moved in on May 22, his birthday. He named the estate "Wahnfried," meaning literally "peace from illusion" but actually signifying that there Wagner would find a refuge from the senseless interruptions and distractions of the world's sordid business.

The house, in the style of an Italian villa, is of yellow brick and rather hideous. Its proportions are pompous rather than graceful, and its pretentiousness is not diminished by a large allegorical panel over the door, the meaning of which, even with Wagner's explanation, baffles the spectator. In a garden plot before the entrance stands a bronze bust of King Ludwig II, which Wagner flattered the monarch into giving him, along with twenty-five thousand dollars for furnishings. The interior decoration is an outstanding example of the clutter fashionable in the 1870's but somewhat depressing today.

Here gathered the Nibelungbureau, a group of young musicians who worshiped Wagner. They copied the score of *The Ring* for the singers and orchestra members, and learned to interpret the music as conductors. Among them were such later famous conductors as Anton Seidl, Felix Mottl, and Hermann Zumpe. With plenty of other members of King Wagner's court they whipped the preparations for the festival, now scheduled for 1876, into a whirlwind of activity.

Wagner was in the thick of the activity—finding singers, a stage designer and a firm to execute his designs, a stage director and stage technicians, and raising more money. The labor and worry told on Wagner's nerves. He would seethe with rage against the uncomprehending Germans with whom he had to deal, and lash out at Cosima with no provocation on her part. Cosima took these outbursts meekly, having learned from living with her mother and father and with Hans von Bülow that existence with a genius is no featherbed.

Around noon on November 21, 1874, Wagner wrote the last notes of *The Twilight of the Gods*, twenty-six years after he had finished the dramatic poem, then called "Siegfried's Death," which was the origin of *The Ring*. Cosima came into his study to bring him the daily newspaper, and found him in a deep reverie. Not wishing to interrupt his thought or to look over his shoulder at his work—something Wagner hated—she stole away without a word. Wagner burst into a fury at what he interpreted as Cosima's lack of interest. Cosima's heart was almost broken by his accusations, but as soon as his flood of anger subsided, Richard took her in his arms and, begging her forgiveness, declared that the reason they suffered so much was that they loved each other too much. On the following day they celebrated the completion of the stupendous work.

Still more money was needed to launch the festival. In 1875, Wagner set out again to try to earn it by concerts. He also supervised productions of *Tannhäuser* and *Lohengrin* in Vienna, and, in March, 1876, of the first performance of *Tristan and Isolde* in Berlin. In December, 1875, the Committee for the Celebration of the Centennial of American Independence asked Wagner to compose a march for the occasion, offering him five thousand dollars for the music. This, and an equivalent sum from the Berlin *Tristan,* brought the festival funds close enough to the total required for it to be definitely scheduled for the summer of 1876 and for contracts to be given to singers and orchestra players.

Rehearsals of the principal singers had taken place during three months of the summer of 1875 in the completed theater. Wagner worked over every detail with these artists, whether it was the enunciation and proper stress of the words, the actual projection of the notes, or a bodily gesture. Wagner persuaded Georg Unger, whom he had chosen for Siegfried, to cancel all engagements for a year in order to remodel his voice for the role and learn the style of acting Wagner demanded. "Your whole outlook on life," Wagner told him, "seems to be too heavy and black; it should become gay and sunny." Wagner actually refashioned this thirty-eight-year-old tenor's entire personality.

The orchestra numbered 115 members, sixty-four of whom were string players. Wagner seated them in a different pattern from usual, with the result that the blending of their tones was refined and mellow. With both the orchestral and singing performers, he stressed melody rather than mere sound.

The acoustics of the new theater, the Festspielhaus, proved to be superb. Wagner at last had an orchestra hidden from the audience. The orchestra pit of the Festspielhaus is ingeniously constructed under the apron of the huge stage, which only the conductor can see. The auditorium seats surround the stage in a fan-shaped semicircle of tiers—another innovation—which rise to the boxes and a gallery at the rear. This "Princes'" gallery, holding about a hundred people, has an entrance of its own; it was designed to satisfy Ludwig II's craving for solitude, especially when listening to one of Wagner's works. The fifteen hundred-odd seats for the public are not upholstered, and are so straight that they can become extremely uncomfortable. Wagner expected concentration, not comfort, on the part of his audiences, but did not seem to recognize that the two are interdependent.

The columned interior of the Festspielhaus is singularly bare of decoration; only a stylized design on the ceiling. This stark appearance was intentional in order to save money; ornament was to be added later, but never was. The orange-colored exterior of brick with white-stone trim is in the nineteenth-century version of the classical style, and, like Wahnfried, is rather more ponderous than the ancient Greeks, who invented the style, intended. Its situation, however, on the top of a small hill at the north end of the city of Bayreuth, is commanding, especially the approach by Siegfried-Wagner-Allee through Richard-Wagner-Park.

Today this park is handsomely landscaped, with fine trees and a charming swan-pond, and the terraces around the Festspielhaus are covered with beautiful flower-beds. In a rose garden to the right is a monumental bronze bust of Wagner. Two restaurants on either side of the theater can accommodate all the patrons, who must take their seats before four P.M., when the festival performances begin.

The streets in the fairly modern section of Bayreuth around the Festspielhaus are named for Wagnerian characters: Lohengrinstrasse, Isoldestrasse, Wotanstrasse, Kundryweg, etc. In the city proper are a Richard-Wagner-Strasse, an important avenue, and a Cosima-Wagner-Strasse.

The personnel of the festival began arriving in Bayreuth in late April, 1876. Rehearsals began in May. The performers and the machinists were generally cooperative, but their occasional bursts of temperament greatly tried the overworked nerves of the indefatigable director, Richard Wagner. And, of course, the scenic effects gave no end of trouble in themselves and to the singer-actors who had to manipulate them or be manipulated by them. The only member of the company who seems to have given no trouble at all was Brünnhilde's horse. The worst blow was the arrival of the intricately articulated dragon from London, minus a neck; that section had apparently been addressed to Beirut, Syria (now Lebanon).

Ludwig II came to a general rehearsal of *The Ring* on August 6, arriving in the utmost secrecy and witnessing the work in almost total privacy. He left Bayreuth on August 9, immediately after *The Twilight of the Gods* rehearsal. "Fortunate century," he declared to Wagner afterward, "that saw this spirit arise in its midst! How future generations will envy those to whom fell the incomparable happiness of being your contemporaries." Ludwig returned for the last public performance.

The first cycle of performances for the public began on August 13 and lasted through August 17. They were repeated four times. After the final curtain fell, on August 30, Wagner addressed the frantically enthusiastic audience: "You have just seen what we can do. Now it rests with you. If you wish it, we shall have an art!"

The festival audience of 1876 were the first to witness any production of *Siegfried* and *The Twilight of the Gods*. Of the four music dramas of *The Ring, Siegfried* is probably the least satisfactory, largely because it is the least integrated. The twelve-year gap between Wagner's composition of the first two acts and of the third split the work both in intention and in style.

The first two acts contain some brilliant music, such as Siegfried's forge song, the orchestral passage of the "Forest Murmurs," and the music of the forest bird. These long acts are truly interesting, however, only in an historical sense; even so, the data they give are overdetailed, and repetitious to anyone who has understood the previous two music dramas in the cycle, and will presently hear much of the same data summarized in *The Twilight of the Gods*. Furthermore, the squabbling between Siegfried and Mime, Mime and Alberich, and Mime and the Wanderer (Wotan) is hardly edifying.

On the other hand, the music with which Wagner characterizes the mean and vicious Mime is monotonous; it is too literal a rendition of Mime's craven, whining nature. So is the boisterous music of Siegfried, who appears in the first two acts less as a hero than as a noisy, unkind, and essentially boring practical joker. The music for Fafner the dragon is obviously intended to be terrifying, but turns out rather ludicrous. The only truly subtle passages are those expressing Mime's rage as he unwittingly gives away his secret thoughts or, as may be, Siegfried reads his mind thanks to the magic gift of the dragon's blood. Big strong Siegfried's murder of the insignificant dwarf Mime seems revoltingly and unnecessarily cruel.

The third act is poetry and music of an entirely different quality. Siegfried's awakening of Brünnhilde, her greeting to the daylight and the world, her magnificent reluctance to yield to her passion, and her final submission to it are expressed in thrilling and exalting music. Brünnhilde appears even greater than in *The Valkyrie*, and Siegfried has suddenly matured into a believable hero and an irresistible lover.

The Twilight of the Gods is the most psychologically complicated of all the music dramas of *The Ring*. All the major characters are human; even Brünnhilde has been deprived of her divine nature. They act and interact as human beings, having no supernatural means at their disposal. The only device is the magic Tarnhelm, the intrusion of which into the plot is unfortunate; today's audiences can take Hagen's brainwashing and memory-restoring drugs as less of a theatrical trick.

Consequently, the music is less grandiose than that of the dramas which are chiefly concerned with gods and goddesses. Perhaps for that reason it is more interesting and more sympathetic. Wagner is infinitely subtle in expressing the changing feelings of his human characters and the contrasts among them. One of his greatest achievements is his revelation of the evil, scheming, hypocritical, and yet strangely ingratiating Hagen, one of the most commanding of all villains. At the other extreme, and equally commanding is Brünnhilde. She is seen first ecstatic with love for Siegfried, next puzzled and disappointed, then furious with rage at the deception that she finds has been practiced upon her, finally destroying herself and the gods who have been responsible for her woe.

In *The Twilight* Wagner is a skillful dramatist, using every opportunity for irony to its fullest advantage. He plays the characters off against one another: the noble Brünnhilde and the simple-minded Gutrune; the bold Siegfried and the timorous Gunther. He varies the stark tragedy with scenes of pathos, such as Waltraute's description of the lonely, grieving Wotan; and to these he contrasts sinister scenes, such as Alberich's mesmerizing of the half-asleep Hagen to avenge him.

Here also Wagner's orchestral passages reach a new peak of emotional expressiveness, such as the exuberant joy and hope of Siegfried's Rhine Journey, the somber melancholy of Siegfried's Funeral March, and the final moments when the waters of the Rhine rise to quench the embers of Brünnhilde's funeral pyre and the gold is at last restored to its rightful owners and peace can come to the troubled world.

The Ring ends as it began, with nature finally vindicated as the controller of human destinies. The problem of desire and greed has been solved by redeeming love—the elemental force of life—in its true form of selflessness.

Wagner had at last brought his dream ship into

harbor. The emperor of Germany, who attended the festival in Bayreuth on August 13 and 14, 1876, was moved to say to him: "I never thought you would bring it off!" But Wagner saw in the first festival only an approximation of what he had intended. Exhausted and disappointed, he left Bayreuth for a rest in Italy.

Even before the kings and emperors—Dom Pedro of Brazil as well as Kaiser William I attended the festival—had left Bayreuth, and the town had returned to its customary placidity, the sordid task of balancing the festival budget began. It soon was apparent that there would be a deficit, which eventually reached the sum of $37,500, a staggering figure for those days. The management committee let the composer know that he was expected to find the money to make up this deficit.

Wagner appealed to the Kaiser and to King Ludwig for support of a new plan of financing future festivals, but neither responded. By the end of 1876 he was ready to declare the undertaking bankrupt, to dispose of the property and equipment, to sell Wahnfried for the benefit of the creditors, sacrifice part of his private income, and also turn over Cosima's recent inheritance from her mother. His flickering faith in the German people almost expired. The only chance he could see for paying the deficit was to sell *The Ring* to other German theaters instead of keeping it, as he had hoped to do, exclusively for Bayreuth.

Early in 1877 an ambitious firm of agents in London proposed to Wagner a series of twenty concerts to be conducted by him in the ten-thousand-seat Albert Hall. The scheme was later reduced to six concerts, for which Wagner would get $7,500, providing the concerts earned that much. Tired though he was, and hating London as he did, Wagner nevertheless accepted the offer as a means of reducing the Bayreuth deficit.

Wagner engaged German singers at high fees for the concerts which were designed to trace his musical development from *Rienzi* to *The Twilight of the Gods*, including his recently composed marches, which even Wagner admitted were inferior products. He and Cosima spent five weeks in London, in May and June, 1877, meeting many of the literary and musical celebrities of England, and being entertained at luncheon by Queen Victoria. The concerts were a critical and social success, but the agents had apparently forgotten that some three thousand of Albert Hall seats were private property and could not be sold. Wagner's income from the series was less than half of what he had been led to expect.

Wagner was now the most internationally admired composer of all time. What grieved and offended and disgusted him was the lack of faith his own nation had in his national theater at Bayreuth. He announced that he would leave ungrateful Germany forever, and settle in America; he had had an offer of a concert tour there.

Since Wagner's egoism had always kept him from accepting any point of view different from his own—and his egoism had by now approached a psychosis—he could not understand the rather sound economic reasoning of the German princes and people that Bayreuth was an unsound proposition financially. Wagner was proud that the princes had come to him in Bayreuth instead of ordering him to their courts as sovereigns had been accustomed to summon musicians in times past. But for all his enthusiasm for the new national feeling in Germany, Wagner could not seem to grasp that there was a new economics involved in it. The age was a frankly materialistic one, preferring to invest in a growing concern than to support a losing one. Nearly a hundred years would pass before a bank or a business would think it advisable for the sake of prestige and public service to subsidize a cultural institution, as an airline company did in 1966 in making a grant for a new production of *The Ring* in New York. To the financiers of the later nineteenth century, prestige meant profits.

King Ludwig II was horrified at learning of Wagner's "frightful idea" of abandoning Germany. "For myself," he wrote to "the Fatherland's greatest genius," "the grief would be so overwhelming as to poison, nay, destroy for ever, my joy in life."

This letter of July, 1877, disclosed to Wagner that he had again touched Ludwig II's weak spot. Wagner hastened to send the monarch a manuscript copy made by Cosima of the dramatic poem of *Parsifal,* which Wagner had begun on January 25, 1877, and completed on April 19.

Wagner had been brooding on the theme of Parsifal as early as 1857. In 1865, he had outlined to King Ludwig the opera he hoped to write on the subject, and prepared a sketch of it. The king had responded with religious enthusiasm. He saw himself even more as Parsifal than he had identified himself with Lohengrin, Parsifal's son. Over the past twelve years he had many times written Wagner of his hopes that soon the composer would return to the subject of Parsifal. He kept referring to himself in letters as Parsifal—a kind of secret code name that was well understood by the correspondents but presumably mysterious to cabinet officials.

Wagner's timing was shrewd. Ludwig, seeing that his dream of producing a *Parsifal* might soon be realized, instructed his minister of finance to develop some plan to rescue Wagner from the burden of the Bayreuth deficit. By March 31, 1878, an arrangement had been worked out whereby Wagner would release *The Ring* to the king's theater in Munich and Wagner's liabilities would be transferred to the Bavarian state.

In 1877, Wagner had regained from Ludwig II the theatrical rights to *The Ring,* which had been granted the king in 1864. The principle of the 1864 agreement was that income from productions of the four music dramas in Munich would repay the king for the allowance Ludwig had granted Wagner and the other sums he had given or advanced to him. Those sums had been made up; Ludwig's investment had proved sound. By the German law of June 11, 1870, Wagner was entitled to royalties from performances of his works, and he needed royalties from *The Ring* in his difficulties after the Bayreuth Festival had proved a financial disaster. Consequently, Wagner licensed the separate parts of *The Ring* to various German theaters, and after 1877 they were frequently given not only in Germany but also in Belgium, Holland, Switzerland, Italy, Hungary, Austria, Russia, and England.

The bickering Wagner had been forced to engage in as a result of the Bayreuth deficit drove him for refuge to *Parsifal.* He prophesied that that work would be his "final victory over life," for he seemed to know that it would be his last work.

After leaving London on June 4, 1877, Wagner had had to go to the health resort of Bad Ems, near Koblenz, in order to recover from new attacks of his old digestive troubles. His erysipelas also returned to plague him. The Bayreuth climate gave him catarrh, and this gave him insomnia. He lived in fear that his heart would give out. The deterioration of his health, largely due to his exertions during the six years preceding the festival of 1876, made his outbursts of temper more frequent and more violent. He was well and in good spirits only when he could lose himself in the ideal, spiritual world of *Parsifal*. In that world, as one of the characters sings, "Space and Time are one."

Since the completion of *Tristan and Isolde* in 1859, Wagner had gradually forsaken his belief in Schopenhauer's pessimistic philosophy and in Oriental mysticism, and had become more and more of a Christian. *Parsifal* was to be his confession of religion, his expression of his own variety of Christianity. He now saw that not renunciation but positive love would be the salvation of the world.

Wagner had always been a Protestant. As George Bernard Shaw pointed out, Siegfried is the perfect example of the Protestant hero. Siegfried, of course, like any other created figure, is a projection of at least a part of the creator's character. Siegfried represents Wagner's rebellion against obsolescent dogmas and hypocrisy. He trusts in his own independent will and intelligence to produce the welfare of society. Wagner's religion was not based on the dogmas of established churches but on the sense of compassion his personal experiences had cultivated in him.

Ruthlessly egoistic himself, Wagner had come to see the destructiveness of that quality. This is not to say that he changed his own conduct accordingly; rather, he seemed to be using his personal experiences as an example to others of what not to be. It is not a unique attitude; compare, for example, the Skid Row bum preaching the evils of drink to other bums in a sheltering mission.

In *The Ring*, which dates from his revolutionary period, Wagner had dramatized the destruction of the world order through greed for power. Indeed, *The Ring* may be interpreted as an allegory of exploitation of the poor by the rich. Now, after Wagner had achieved what he had dreamed of, he was bitterly disappointed, a common reaction with him.

Wagner had lost faith in the German spirit he had helped to bring alive. He saw it now as barbarous, and the German state as incapable of culture because it had not responded to his call to salvation through art. "This new Germany disgusts me," he wrote to a friend, referring to the arrogant, warlike character that the German Empire had acquired since 1870. He recognized that in his reconstruction of the old German myths, he had prophesied the destruction of Germany itself.

Wagner, however, could not live in passive contemplation of such a dreary end for Germany or for himself. If the old gods were to have a twilight, there must be a dawn to follow it. Wagner had already glimpsed that dawn in his own experiences. These had led him to a mystical interpretation of them. The benevolence of King Ludwig II, for example, he conceived as proof that God protects and cares for those who have a message from Him to give to His world.

Old and sick and troubled by the thought that he had frequently behaved in an antisocial way, Wagner yearned for forgiveness. King Ludwig II had forgiven him for behavior that was deceptive, if not downright dishonest. Wagner believed that the king's pity on his human frailties was a token of Jesus' compassion on sinful mortals. He found the very thought of Jesus restoring his hope of salvation. Surely, Wagner trusted, Jesus would forgive him. He began to believe in the power of prayer to procure for him the redemption through Jesus' intercession and God's love that he had once thought could come only through a woman's self-sacrifice.

All these reversals of attitude, these new mystical thoughts and feelings, Wagner wished to express in *Parsifal*. *Parsifal* would place in men's hearts a knowledge of Christ. This would make a bright new day for the world, following the night that had swallowed up the old gods. Parsifal would succeed in redeeming the world, whereas Siegfried had failed. Parsifal would renounce passion for the sake of eternal life, whereas Tristan had renounced life for the sake of passion. Parsifal's quest for the Holy Grail, the symbol of Christ's redeeming sacrifice for the world, would be transformed into music, the language of the soul. The music would, therefore, rescue the soul from destruction by replacing vengeance with compassion.

Compassion became Wagner's personal quest. He deplored the fate of the small nations that Germany was threatening with conquest or obliteration. He even took up the cause of antivivisection, and advocated vegetarianism. His sense of guilt drove him to preach the preservation of all forms of life as relentlessly as once he had preached the pessimism of Schopenhauer.

The intensity of Wagner's feeling for *Parsifal* spilled over into his personal life. He had scarcely begun to compose the music in August, 1877, than he began a correspondence with the beautiful Judith Gautier, with whom he had had a momentary romance when she came to Bayreuth for the festival of 1876. Wagner persuaded himself that he was in love with her. She does not seem to have taken him very seriously—he was thirty-seven years older than she—and Cosima certainly did not take seriously Wagner's "exquisite intoxication," as he called it.

It was all a part of Wagner's necessity to isolate himself from the ugly world of reality. Judith helped by sending him (via the Bayreuth barber to avoid scandal) the perfumes, bath salts, cold creams, and silks he asked her to get for him in Paris. "I have three years' work at *Parsifal* before me," he wrote her, "and nothing must tear me away from the sweet peace of creative isolation." But once *Parsifal* was fairly launched, Wagner sobered up and broke off the correspondence.

Wagner's health made it advisable for him to be as much as possible in a warmer climate than Bayreuth's. He spent a great deal of time in Italy. In Palermo,

Sicily, he finished the orchestration of *Parsifal* on January 13, 1882. A performance was scheduled for the summer of 1882 at Bayreuth.

On Wagner's entreaty, King Ludwig had released his right by the agreement of March 31, 1878, to produce *Parsifal* in Munich. Wagner could not bear the thought of that religious music drama, his personal confession of faith, becoming just another opera in the repertory of a commercial theater. It must be, Wagner insisted, a "*Sacred* Dramatic Festival." Ludwig II guaranteed seventy-five thousand dollars for a production in the Festspielhaus, and also contributed the services of the Munich theater's chorus and orchestra.

Wagner abandoned the previous system of patrons whose subscriptions were supposedly to finance the festivals at Bayreuth. He opened the *Parsifal* festival to the general public at $7.50 a ticket. The money flowed in for the sixteen performances of *Parsifal*, beginning on July 26 and continuing through August 29, 1882.

Being a religious music drama, *Parsifal*'s story can be truly appreciated only by the religious. To those who have never been initiated by training and practice into the mysteries of religion, it can be exasperatingly perplexing. Wagner's egoism and the intensity of his religious feeling in 1877 led him, otherwise an experienced and skillful dramatist, into the error of thinking that he could make mystical personages interesting on the stage. His characters, therefore, are not clearly motivated, and end up as bores if for no other reason than that they have to talk too much in order for the audience even to glimpse what they want or do not want. The result is that *Parsifal* is terribly long-winded.

The music of *Parsifal* is not so easy to dismiss. True, it is usually solemn and painfully slow, often lacking in invention and sometimes as obvious as that accompanying a meretricious motion picture (for example, Amfortas' confession in the final scene). On the other hand, Wagner surpassed himself in the tone painting of the Flower Maidens' scene. One can almost literally see the colors of the flowers, smell their perfume, feel their soft blossoms. But the music is truly at its best when no pseudohuman beings intrude to break the spell—the great choral music of the scenes in the Temple of the Holy Grail, the orchestral passages of the Prelude and the Good Friday scene, the processions, and the transitional passages that cover the scene shifting.

In general, the music accomplishes just what Wagner intended it to do—elevate the soul to an understanding of compassion and love. It is exalted music that evokes whatever faith its listeners have in the reality of things not seen.

On the evening of August 31, 1882, Wagner suffered the worst of the several heart attacks he had recently experienced. He recovered sufficiently to leave Bayreuth on September 14 for Venice, where, in the previous spring, he had rented the Palazzo Vendramin for the coming winter. There he lived quietly, writing articles for the newspaper he had founded in 1878 as propaganda for the Bayreuth festival. On the afternoon of February 13, 1883, he suffered a violent heart attack, and expired in Cosima's arms.

Wagner's body was brought home to Bayreuth by train. Along the way it was given royal honors. Wagner was buried in the garden behind Wahnfried at twilight on February 18, 1883.

Appendix

THE STORIES OF WAGNER'S OPERAS

CHARACTERS

(in order of appearance)

PAOLO ORSINI, head of the Orsini family
IRENE DI RIENZI, sister of Cola di Rienzi
STEFANO COLONNA, head of the Colonna family
ADRIANO, his son
CARDINAL RAIMUNDO, papal legate
COLA DI RIENZI, appointee of Pope Clement VI to end the civil strife in Rome
CECCO, a blacksmith, spokesman of the Roman people
BARONCELLI, a demagogue

The scene is Rome, about 1350.

BACKGROUND

With the seat of the papacy transferred to Avignon, where the popes are political pawns of the French king, and with Rome under the domination of the German emperor, the holy city has become a battleground for the rivalry of powerful noble families, each of which maintains an army of followers in their fortress-palaces. The people of Rome have suffered greatly from this turbulence. Cola di Rienzi, who dreams of reestablishing the glory of ancient Rome as a free republic, has gone to the pope in Avignon, who has appointed him apostolic notary with a mission to put an end to the misrule of the nobles in Rome.

ACT I

In the dark of night, Paolo Orsini and his armed retinue are in the process of kidnaping Irene di Rienzi from her brother's house. Her screams for help arouse the Colonna troop. In the street skirmish between these rival factions, Adriano Colonna rescues Irene. The Roman people, Cola di Rienzi's party, join the tumult, and refuse to disperse when urged by Cardinal Raimundo. Rienzi, however, is a strong enough leader to get them to stop the brawling. The rival noblemen agree to fight it out on the following day outside the city walls. Rienzi decides to close the gates on them and keep them out of the city until they have sworn to keep the peace. He calls on the people to rally to him after the nobles have been locked out, and to defend the freedom of Rome.

Rienzi now discovers that the cause of the riot was his own sister and that her rescuer is one of his deadliest enemies. He plays upon the friendship that he and Adriano enjoyed as children to persuade the young man to join the people's party. Adriano remains in Rienzi's house to protect Irene, with whom he is in love.

At sunrise, Rienzi rings the great bell of the Capitol to announce the beginning of the revolution that will deliver the Roman people from the tyranny of the nobles. There follows a great procession, with the people cheering Rienzi and swearing their loyalty to him.

ACT II

The nobles, having taken the required oath, meet with Rienzi in the Capitol, where, much to their disgust, they learn of the general support of Rienzi throughout the land. The nobles plot to assassinate Rienzi.

Adriano reveals this conspiracy to Rienzi, and the attempt at murder fails. The people, led by Cecco, demand the execution of the conspirators. Rienzi is about to consent, but Irene and Adriano implore him to show mercy, for, of course, Adriano's father would otherwise be beheaded as a major conspirator. The nobles are forgiven in exchange for their promise to obey the revolutionary government Rienzi has set up, but they have no intention of keeping their word.

ACT III

In a public square of Rome, the people are discussing the escape of the nobles from the city, which they are preparing to reenter with their forces and destroy the new republic. Adriano, trapped between loyalty to his father and loyalty to Rienzi, begs Rienzi to try conciliation again. But Rienzi marches at the head of the people's army, chanting their war song, "Santo Spirito Cavaliere," to crush the nobles at the gates.

ACT IV

The defeated nobles are now trying to destroy Rienzi through intrigue with the pope and the emperor. Outside the Church of St. John Lateran, Baroncelli and Cecco inflame the Roman people with the false report that Rienzi's poor leadership is to blame for the pope and the emperor having gone over to the nobles' side. Adriano, smitten with guilt over his father's death in battle, vows that he will kill Rienzi. The fickle people now turn against Rienzi as passionately as once they upheld him. The cardinal, however, summons them into the church for a Te Deum in celebration of Rienzi's victory over their oppressors.

Rienzi marches to that service with Irene and his bodyguard. Just as they are about to enter the church, the cardinal emerges and excommunicates Rienzi for allegedly conspiring against the pope. Irene refuses to leave her outlawed brother for Adriano, and Rienzi swears that he will continue the struggle for Roman freedom from domination by pope, emperor, and nobles.

ACT V

In the Capitol, Rienzi prays for God's protection

on his city and its misguided people. He begs Irene to leave him, but she refuses to do so, even though her loyalty will lose her Adriano's love. She encourages Rienzi to make a last stand to control his beloved Rome.

Adriano pleads with Irene to flee with him before the enraged people burn down the Capitol with Rienzi and her in it. But he succeeds in dragging her away and her in it. But only after she has fainted from the smoke that has begun to billow through the building does he succeed in dragging her away. Baroncelli and Cecco drown out Rienzi's final appeal to the Romans. The Capitol collapses upon him.

The Flying Dutchman

(*Der Fliegende Holländer*)

CHARACTERS

(in order of appearance)

DALAND, a Norwegian skipper
STEERSMAN of Daland's ship
THE DUTCHMAN*
MARY, Senta's old nurse
SENTA, Daland's daughter
ERIK, a hunter, engaged to Senta
Norwegian sailors, Senta's girl companions, the crew of the Dutchman's vessel

The scene is the seacoast of Norway around the fishing village of Sandvika, near Oslo. The time is presumably the then present, that is, around 1840.

ACT I

Daland's ship has been blown off course to Sandvika, a short distance from his own village. He has just anchored there when into the harbor sails a mysterious

* In some versions of the story he is called Vanderdecken. Wagner claimed in his autobiography that he learned of the legend of the Flying Dutchman from the sailors on the ship that took him from Germany to England in 1839. He had, however, read Heinrich Heine's version of the story, and possibly some of the many other literary versions current at that time. The story was a common and popular piece of folklore in the Romantic period.

vessel with black masts and blood-red canvas. Ashore steps its sinister captain, dressed in a black costume of the sixteenth century. In a monologue he tells of his strange fate. Because of a curse upon him he must sail the seas until he finds a woman who will love him enough to sacrifice herself for him. Only once every seven years, as now, may he go on land in search of her. He yearns for this love which will at last allow him to die.

Daland welcomes the Dutchman, who asks for shelter and proves by the treasure his ship contains that he can well reward his host. When the wind shifts, the greedy Daland conducts the Dutchman to his house, where, Daland strongly hints, he will find a fine girl—Daland's daughter Senta—for a wife.

ACT II

In Daland's house, Senta's girl companions have gathered for a spinning bee. Senta's old nurse Mary rebukes her for not working at her spinning wheel to make herself a trousseau, but Senta just continues to gaze at the portrait of a sinister man in a black, sixteenth-century costume. She sings a ballad of the Flying Dutchman, after which she announces that she herself is the one who, given the chance, would redeem the unlucky captain from his curse.

Mary and the girls are horrified at Senta's outburst, and so is Erik, who has entered in time to hear it. Erik pleads with Senta to be faithful to him, and not to yield to her father's desire to marry her to a richer man. He recounts a dream in which Senta gave herself to a stranger whom her father brought home, a man much like the portrait on the wall. Senta has gone into a kind of trance during Erik's narration, and even sees the climax of his story before he reaches it. At its end, she declares that she will risk her life for the stranger.

At that moment, Daland and the Dutchman enter. Daland urges Senta to welcome his guest, and bribes her to become the Dutchman's wife by showing her some of the jewelry that the Dutchman will give her. Then Daland leaves them alone to get acquainted. Senta and the Dutchman recognize that they have somehow been always destined for each other, and Senta vows her eternal fidelity to him.

ACT III

Down at the harbor, the Norwegian sailors and the Norwegian girls are merrily starting in on the wedding party that Daland is giving for Senta and the Dutchman. A mysterious storm agitates the Dutch ship, but does not disturb the Norwegian vessel moored alongside it. The cynical Dutch crew appear to prophesy the usual disappointing end to their holiday on land.

Erik reminds Senta of all he had once meant to her and of how she had promised to be faithful to him.

The Dutchman, who has overheard the last part of Erik's plea that Senta remember her vows, and misunderstands it, cries, "All is lost!" He boards his ship and prepares to sail away for another seven years of wandering. Senta tears herself away from Daland, Erik, and Mary, and, rushing to a rock that overhangs the shore, throws herself into the sea.

The spectral Dutch ship, with all on board, sinks into a whirlpool. Then, as the sun sets, the forms of Senta and the Dutchman, in a close embrace, appear rising from the water and ascending skyward.

CHARACTERS

(in order of appearance)

VENUS, goddess of youth, beauty, and sensuous love

TANNHÄUSER (*Tahn*-hoy-zer), a minnesinger, that is, an aristocratic medieval German poet-singer of courtly love—a formalized poetry dealing with the love of a prince for an unattainable princess, derived from the religious love and worship of the Virgin Mary. He is sometimes addressed as Heinrich (Henry).

A SHEPHERD

LANDGRAF HERMANN, the feudal ruler of Thuringia

WOLFRAM VON ESCHENBACH
WALTHER VON DER VOGELWEIDE
BITEROLF
HEINRICH DER SCHREIBER
REIMAR VON ZWEITER
} minnesingers

ELIZABETH, niece of Landgraf Hermann

Venus' nymphs; pilgrims; Thuringian nobles and their ladies

The scene is the region around Eisenach, in Thuringia, about the year 1200.

ACT I

In the luxurious grotto where Venus holds her court

of sensuous love, Tannhäuser is being entertained by the riotous revels of Venus' staff of bacchantes, fauns, satyrs, sirens, and nymphs—and atmospheric tableaux representing several of the famous love stories of classic mythology.

As this erotic pageantry ends, Tannhäuser reveals his discontent with the long stay he has enjoyed in this magic land of fleshly pleasure. He yearns to return to the real world of men, and save his soul by devoting himself to religion. In spite of Venus' amorous pleading with him to remain her captive, Tannhäuser sees that her allure is a poor substitute for the eternal, forgiving love of the Virgin. "My hope is in Mary," he exclaims.

At the mention of that holy name, the grotto vanishes, and Tannhäuser finds himself in the sunny valley beneath the castle-crowned Wartburg near Eisenach. A shepherd is singing of the beauty of May, the month of Mary, ironically connecting her with Holda (that is, Venus in northern mythology), the goddess of spring.

A band of pilgrims on their way to Rome, singing of their hope of salvation, move Tannhäuser to a prayer of thankfulness for his deliverance from servitude to Venus. While he is kneeling before the wayside shrine of the Virgin, Landgraf Hermann and his troop of minnesingers return from hunting. They welcome Tannhäuser after his long absence, which he does not explain. He consents to remain with them only after

Wolfram tells him how Elizabeth, who now lives at the Wartburg, has missed him. The whole retinue move off to that castle, singing their joy that their beloved brother has returned, no more to stray.

ACT II

Elizabeth consecrates the Hall of Song in the Wartburg castle for the contest of poetry and music that is about to take place there. She greets Tannhäuser tenderly; his return has renewed her life with the blessed power of love.

Landgraf Hermann invites Tannhäuser to join the contest, even though Tannhäuser still refuses to tell where he has been. The Landgraf announces that the theme of the contest is love, what it is and how it can be recognized.

Wolfram begins the contest with a poem glorifying pure and holy love. To this Tannhäuser responds with his entry, a song in praise of fleshly love. Biterolf denounces him as a shameless blasphemer, and challenges him to combat. The Landgraf restrains them, in spite of the nobles' disgust with Tannhäuser, and Wolfram invokes the aid of heaven to keep the subject matter pure, "fanned by an angel's wing."

Tannhäuser, however, is swept away by his memory of his years with Venus, and bursts into a passionate extolling of the joys of physical ardor.

The horrified women withdraw in mortification,

and the nobles draw their swords on Tannhäuser. Now they know that he has been in unholy Venus' thrall. They curse him for defaming their sacred tournament with his foul presence, and demand his exile.

Elizabeth, however, protects Tannhäuser with her body. She maintains that he must be given the opportunity to redeem his soul; it is not for them to judge him, for only God may do that.

Seeing the justice of Elizabeth's argument, the Landgraf spares Tannhäuser's life on condition that the erring minnesinger go to Rome to seek pardon from the pope. Tannhäuser, who really wants his soul—not to mention his life—to be saved, consents to join a band of young pilgrims on their way to Rome.

ACT III

In the autumn twilight, Elizabeth is praying before the shrine in the valley beneath the Wartburg when a band of pilgrims pass by on their way back from Rome, chanting the famous Pilgrims' Chorus, "Once more, dear home, I with rapture behold thee!" Finding no Tannhäuser among them, Elizabeth renews her prayers that she may leave this world of care still pure, and that Tannhäuser may achieve salvation.

Wolfram, who has been watching her, prays that Tannhäuser may return to ease her longing, even though, in that event, he himself will have loved the holy Elizabeth in vain. Left alone, Wolfram, in his

"Song to the Evening Star," prays that Elizabeth may be welcomed in heaven as a star of equally pure light, which will illumine the souls of mortals.

Tannhäuser, now old and worn, totters along. The pope has refused him absolution until the pontiff's staff shall put forth green leaves; therefore, Tannhäuser intends to return to Venus' realm, if only he can find the way again. As Wolfram tries to dissuade him from this recidivism, Venus appears, welcoming Tannhäuser back to her embraces. Wolfram insists that Tannhäuser's soul can still be saved because of Elizabeth's prayers. At the mention of that sainted name, Venus vanishes; she has lost Tannhäuser again.

Men from the Wartburg bring in the bier of the just deceased Elizabeth and place it before the shrine, declaring that Tannhäuser can indeed be saved because now Elizabeth will intercede for him in heaven. With a prayer to the new saint, Tannhäuser expires by her body.

At that moment, the band of young pilgrims appear, carrying the pope's staff, which has miraculously blossomed as a sign that Tannhäuser has received pardon for his sins of the flesh from the highest of all authorities.

Lohengrin

CHARACTERS

(in order of appearance)

THE KING'S HERALD

HENRY I, later known as Henry the Fowler, king of Germany

FREDERICK OF TELRAMUND, Count of Brabant

ORTRUD, his wife

ELSA OF BRABANT, Telramund's ward

LOHENGRIN (*Low*-an-green), the Knight of the Swan

DUKE GODFREY OF BRABANT, the rightful heir of Brabant, Elsa's brother

German and Brabantian nobles and their ladies. Court attendants

The scene is Antwerp in Brabant (present-day Belgium) about the year 933.

ACT I

King Henry has come to a meadow on the banks of the river Scheldt to enlist the support of the Brabantians in his campaign against the pagan Huns, who are renewing their warfare against Christianized Germany after a nine years' truce. He finds his Brabantian vassals in a state of civil war because of the mysterious disappearance of the young Duke Godfrey and the usurpation of the duchy by Count Frederick of Telramund, who had once saved the king's life in battle.

Telramund answers the king's investigation by accusing Elsa, his ward, of having done away with her young brother in order to get the duchy for herself. Elsa's father had intended Telramund to marry her, but Telramund, convinced that Elsa is a sorceress, has married the pagan Ortrud instead.

Standing under the oak of justice, the king decrees that this charge of fratricide must be judged by the legal and holy ritual of trial by combat—Telramund against Elsa's champion. When the king orders Elsa to name her defender, she tells of her dream that a knight in shining armor with a horn of gold would appear to prove her innocence. She promises her hand and her inheritance to whoever will fight her cause; if no one fights for her, or if her champion loses, she will accept punishment for her alleged crime.

The herald summons a champion for Elsa to step forward, but for several tense moments no one answers the challenge. Then down the Scheldt River comes a swan-drawn boat in which stands the very image of the defender Elsa had dreamed of.

That knight offers his services to Elsa on the conditions that she will marry him and that she will never ask his name or his origins. In the combat, Telramund falls to the knight, who generously spares his life, as all the people rejoice.

ACT II

Inside the castle of Antwerp, a feast is in progress to celebrate the coming marriage of Elsa and the Knight of the Swan. Outside, in the dark courtyard, Telramund, whom the king has punished by outlawing him, upbraids Ortrud for having induced him to make the false charge against Elsa that now has lost him everything. Ortrud assures her husband that her magic spells will save him yet by ruining the mysterious knight.

Elsa comes to a window overlooking the courtyard, rapturously happy. Ortrud invokes the aid of her pagan gods against Elsa, then pleads with Elsa for forgiveness and protection, which Elsa grants and also invites Ortrud to the wedding. Ortrud's thanks is to insinuate that since the knight appeared as if by magic, Elsa would be wise not to trust him too implicitly.

As day breaks, the courtyard fills with people beginning the celebration of Elsa's marriage to the knight, who has renounced all claim to the duchy but whom the king has named his general in the campaign against the Huns.

As Elsa, escorted by a grand procession, approaches the castle church, Ortrud blocks her way, asserting her rights as the wife of Telramund, the legal duke. No sooner has the knight driven Ortrud away than Telramund blocks the procession, proclaiming that the knight is a sorcerer and demanding his name. The Knight of the Swan refuses to deal with the dishonored Telramund, and asserts that Elsa alone has the right to ask his identity. Telramund then whispers to Elsa that he can help her learn the truth about her betrothed if only she will call for her guardian that very night. The knight orders both Telramund and Ortrud out of his sight forever.

King Henry leads the bridal pair up the steps to the church door. There, as Elsa turns to her knight, she glimpses Ortrud in a gesture of defiance and certain victory.

ACT III, Scene 1

The king and the nobles escort Elsa and her knight into their bridal chamber, singing the famous and joyous Bridal Chorus.

Once they are alone, Elsa longs to be able to speak her bridegroom's name. The doubt Ortrud has planted in her mind begins to grow until Elsa becomes as visionary as she was in Act I and sees the same magic that brought her husband to her taking him away from her. To free her from this fear, he must tell her his name.

At that moment, Telramund and four armed followers break into the room. Suddenly recalled to reality, Elsa shouts to her husband to defend himself, and hands him his sword. The knight strikes Telramund dead. Sadly, the knight then exclaims that his happiness with Elsa is ended. He orders the four men to carry Telramund's corpse to the king, and Elsa's women to prepare her to accompany it, for he will then disclose his identity.

ACT IV, Scene 2

In the meadow under the oak of justice, King Henry waits for his new general to lead the warriors against the foe. Following Telramund's body and Elsa, who is silent with grief over her lack of trust, comes the Knight of the Swan to explain the death of Telramund. The king absolves him of guilt on the grounds of self-defense.

Then the knight informs the people that Elsa having broken her vow, they shall all know who he is. He is Lohengrin, son of Parsifal, the keeper of the Holy Grail in far-off Monsalvat.* From there he has been sent by the power of the Grail to defend the innocent from false charges; to Monsalvat he must now return, for his origin and his identity have been disclosed. Sorrowfully he reproaches Elsa for her weak faith in the power of Heaven to protect her.

The swan appears on the river. Lohengrin gives Elsa his sword, horn, and ring—for her brother, whom the Grail has protected, and who will indeed return—

* Monsalvat (Monserrat) is a high, steep mountain that rises abruptly from a plain about forty miles northwest of Barcelona, Spain.

and prepares to enter the boat the swan has brought for him.

Ortrud breaks through the crowd, shouting that she has triumphed over Elsa. Ortrud confesses that she changed Elsa's brother into the swan that draws the boat; if Elsa had not broken her promise to Lohengrin, he would have transformed the swan back into Duke Godfrey, and Elsa would then have had both her brother and her husband.

The white dove of the Holy Grail descends over Lohengrin's head. Lohengrin loosens the swan from its harness. It sinks, and in its place Lohengrin raises the white-clad Duke Godfrey, whom he proclaims the rightful ruler of Brabant.

The dove takes the chain that draws the boat, and, with Lohengrin aboard, pulls it out of sight. Elsa expires in her brother's arms.

Tristan and Isolde

CHARACTERS

(in order of appearance)

A YOUNG SAILOR (who sings but does not appear in person)
ISOLDE (Iz-*ol*-da), an Irish princess betrothed to King Marke
BRANGAENE (Bran-*gay*-na), her companion and serving-woman
KURWENAL (*Koor*-ven-ahl), Tristan's faithful friend and squire
TRISTAN, nephew of King Marke
KING MARKE OF CORNWALL
MELOT, Tristan's false friend
A SHEPHERD
Sailors, knights, attendants

The scenes are laid on a ship voyaging from Ireland to Cornwall (now a southwestern county of England); in the garden of King Marke's castle in Cornwall; in Tristan's castle in Brittany (the northwestern peninsula of France). The historical time is the sixth century; the legendary time is the twelfth century.

ACT I

Tristan is bringing by ship from Ireland the Princess

Isolde to be the bride of his uncle King Marke. Some time before, Tristan had slain the Irish knight Morold and put an end to his extortions on King Marke. In that encounter, Tristan received a wound so severe that only Isolde, Morold's fiancée, could cure it. Isolde healed Tristan, and in doing so, pierced his disguise. She was preparing to kill him to avenge Morold, when she fell in love with the Cornish hero, and spared him. Later, in order to end the rivalry between Ireland and Cornwall, Isolde's parents arranged her marriage to King Marke without her consent.

Isolde feels disgraced at being handed over by the same Tristan she secretly loves to his weary uncle, who once had to pay tribute money to Morold. Rather than suffer this shame, and lose Tristan, who has ignored her on the voyage out of loyalty to King Marke, Isolde orders Brangaene to prepare a poisoned drink that she will offer Tristan and then consume herself.

Kurwenal bursts into Isolde's cabin to announce that the shore of Cornwall is in sight. Isolde sends him to bring Tristan to her. She offers Tristan the supposedly poisoned cup as a pledge that she has forgotten her wish to avenge Morold and desires to be friendly to her future husband's most trusted knight. Tristan drinks half the cup, then Isolde snatches it from him and drains it.

Brangaene, however, had been unable to bear the thought of her beloved Isolde destroying herself, and had substituted a love potion for the deadly poison. Tristan and Isolde are now irrevocably in love with each other.

The sailors shout, as they drop anchor in Cornwall, that King Marke is about to come on board to claim his bride.

ACT II

In the garden of King Marke's castle, Isolde waits for another rendezvous with Tristan while the king is hunting. Brangaene warns her that this hunt may be a ruse planned by Melot, who she thinks will betray the lovers out of jealousy. Isolde's desire, however, has made her heedless, and she gives the signal for Tristan to come to her.

The lovers revel in the ecstasy of their passion, and long for death to end their separation by uniting them forever.

Suddenly Brangaene cries out that the king is returning, and Kurwenal dashes into the garden to warn Tristan to defend himself.

King Marke is deeply hurt at Tristan's betrayal. Tristan's guilt so overcomes him on the one hand, and Isolde's promise to follow him no matter where so excites him on the other hand, that he sees death as the only way out. Consequently, Tristan makes no defense against the jealous Melot, who attacks him in a pretense at avenging the king's honor and grievously wounds him.

ACT III

The mournful Tristan lies dying in the garden of his desolate castle on the seacoast cliffs of Brittany, yearning for Isolde to come to him. Kurwenal and a shepherd keep watch for the sail that will bring her as she had sworn. Tristan is almost dead of grief and longing when the sail appears.

Tristan leaps from his bed, tearing the bandage from his wound so that Isolde will find him as she did when he sought her cure from Morold's wound. He staggers to meet his beloved, but he is able only to whisper her name before he expires in Isolde's arms. Isolde swoons on Tristan's lifeless body.

The shepherd announces the arrival of a second ship, on board which are King Marke, Melot, and Brangaene. He and Kurwenal rush to shut the gate of the castle against the reprisals Kurwenal expects the king to make. Kurwenal hurls himself at Melot, and kills him; then he attacks the king's men, who wound him mortally. He lurches to Tristan, and dies beside him.

King Marke laments that he has come too late with his forgiveness, for Brangaene has confessed everything to him, and he now understands.

Isolde revives. She sees Tristan already transfigured, open-eyed and smiling, drawing her mystically toward him. Her intense emotion seems to carry her to her lover high amid the stars as she expires in a transport of bliss.

King Marke invokes a blessing on the dead.

The Mastersingers of Nuremberg

(*Die Meistersinger von Nürnberg*)

CHARACTERS

(in order of appearance)

WALTHER VON STOLZING, a young knight of Franconia
EVA (*Aye*-va), Veit Pogner's daughter
MAGDALENA, Eva's maid
DAVID (*Dah*-veed), Hans Sachs's apprentice, in love with Magdalena

Mastersingers:
VEIT POGNER, goldsmith
SIXTUS BECKMESSER, town clerk of Nuremberg
HANS SACHS, cobbler
FRITZ KOTHNER, baker
KUNZ VOGELSANG, furrier
HERMANN ORTEL, soapmaker
BALTHASAR ZORN, pewterer
KONRAD NACHTIGALL, tinsmith
AUGUSTIN MOSER, tailor
ULRICH EISSLINGER, grocer
HANS FOLTZ, coppersmith
HANS SCHWARTZ, stocking-weaver

A NIGHT WATCHMAN
The people of Nuremberg

The scene is Nuremberg in 1560.

ACT I

In Nuremberg's Church of St. Catherine, Walther von Stolzing is flirting with Eva. Once the St. John's Eve service is over, they contrive to be alone.

Walther has visited Nuremberg before, and has stayed at Pogner's house, where he and Eva fell in love. Now, on his return, Walther wants to know whether Eva has become engaged to any man during his absence. Magdalena tells him that Pogner has promised Eva's hand to whoever wins the prize at the Mastersingers' exhibition of their art on the following day, St. John's or Midsummer Day. Walther immediately decides to compete.

David tries to instruct Walther in the complicated rules and regulations of the Mastersingers while their apprentices set up the benches for the trial run of the contest.

As the Mastersingers are assembling, Beckmesser, an elderly bachelor, pleads with Pogner to persuade Eva to look with favor upon him in the coming contest of song, for Pogner has indicated that if Eva is to marry the winner, she shall have the right to choose him.

Pogner then introduces Walther as a candidate for the Mastersinger's company. Sensing a rival for Eva's hand, Beckmesser becomes antagonistic to the handsome young knight. When Walther sings his trial song, Beckmesser, "the marker," or scorer of errors in a poem and its musical rendition, finds so many faults that he demands the exclusion of the knight from the contest.

Hans Sachs, however, has perceived that although Walther's song does not fit the arbitrary and pedantic rules of the Mastersingers, it is a work of genuine and fresh inspiration. He champions Walther, but he is shouted down by the other Mastersingers, and the trial session ends in confusion.

ACT II

Opposite Pogner's house, Hans Sachs moves his cobbler's bench into the cool air of the midsummer night in order to finish Beckmesser's new shoes in time for the next day's festival. Eva comes to inquire how Walther fared in the trial, thus indicating to Sachs where her affections lie. Although the widower Sachs has a great fatherly affection for Eva, and has had some encouragement from her that if he were to sing in the contest she might award him the prize of her hand in marriage, he now resolves not to compete and to fix things so that Walther can sing in the contest after all.

Walther comes to Eva's house to confess his failure at the trial and to urge her to elope with him as the only way in which she can escape her father's decree. Sachs, who has overheard them, plots to prevent such a dishonest plan.

Beckmesser now appears with a lute to serenade Eva, whom he thinks he sees at her window. But the woman there is actually Magdalena in Eva's clothes; Eva and Walther are hiding in the shrubbery by Pogner's front door.

Beckmesser is irritated at finding Sachs cobbling away outside his own house, and also loudly singing a lusty cobbler's song. But Sachs tells him that if he wants his new shoes finished in time, he must not disturb the shoemaker. Go ahead and sing your serenade, Sachs tells the pedantic town clerk, and I'll be marker for you; thus, you will know the mistakes you make and so can correct them in time to give a perfect song and win the prize.

Beckmesser begins his serenade, but is so frequently interrupted by Sachs's hammer indicating mistakes in his banal song that he gets too flustered to sing correctly at all. Just as Sachs is holding up the shoes he has been able to finish thanks to rapping out Beckmesser's errors, David opens his window shutter to discover Beckmesser singing a love song to Magdalena, whom David easily recognizes in spite of her disguise.

Furiously jealous, David rushes out into the street and attacks Beckmesser. The noise of their fighting awakes the neighbors, who arouse others, and presently the street is full of brawlers who don't know what they are really fighting about. The fracas so blocks the street that Eva and Walther cannot get through it to elope.

Walther desperately draws his sword and prepares to hack his way through the mob, but Sachs grabs hold of him. Just then the night watchman's horn is heard, and the squabbling townspeople quickly disperse for fear of arrest. Pogner drags Eva into her house, and Sachs drags Walther into his.

When the night watchman comes along the deserted street, singing his all's-well song, Nuremberg is apparently sleeping soundly in the midsummer moonlight.

ACT III, Scene 1

On the following sunny morning, Hans Sachs is peacefully reading a huge book inside his shop. He humorously forgives David for having started the previous night's riot, and appoints him herald of the forthcoming festivities. Then Sachs ponders the madness that causes every living thing to fall to quarreling as on last night in his beloved Nuremberg. "Now," he says, "we shall see how Hans Sachs can direct this midsummer fever to some noble work."

Walther interrupts Sachs' monologue with the announcement that in a dream he has conceived a song which he begs Sachs to hear. Sachs is deeply moved by the beauty of Walther's lyric, the words of which he writes down as the knight sings them. Sachs sends Walther off to compose a concluding stanza, and follows him in order to dress for the festival.

Bruised and lame from David's beating, Beckmesser limps in while the shop is empty, in order to get his new shoes adjusted. In revenge for the brawl, which Beckmesser thinks was instigated by Sachs, he steals Walther's poem under the belief that it is the one Sachs intends to sing in the contest.

Returning, Sachs shrewdly strengthens this misconception in Beckmesser's mind, and makes him a present of the poem. For Sachs knows that Walther's free and spontaneous lyric is so different from the regulation-bound, artificial verse that Beckmesser is used to that the town clerk will never be able to master it. Beckmesser leaves to memorize his newfound treasure.

Eva comes ostensibly to get her shoe repaired, but, as Sachs recognizes, really to see Walther for the last time. Sachs contrives to leave the lovers alone, then returns to tell Eva that he will not compete, thus leaving the field free for Walther to win her legitimately with his new song which she has inspired. Sachs then frees David from his apprenticeship, and, joined by Magdalena, the four lovers sing of their gratitude and joy, while Hans Sachs adds to the quintet his own slightly rueful resignation of his hope to wed Eva.

ACT III, Scene 2

All the people of Nuremberg have assembled in gala attire on the bank of the Pegnitz River for the Mastersingers' festival. In the bright sunshine they create a pageant of sumptuous costumes, flags and banners and trumpets, music and dancing.

Beckmesser, being the oldest of the contestants, is invited to open the competition. He has been quite unable to memorize the stolen song or to fit a melody to it. Consequently, the harder he tries to render it, the more confused he becomes until he is finally braying pure jargon. The people hoot at him and force him to resign. In rage and humiliation, Beckmesser shouts that the poem is not his but Hans Sachs's.

Sachs protests that all the song needs is to be properly interpreted by its true author, and calls on Walther to sing it. The people are overwhelmed by the exquisite beauty of the poem and its melody. When Walther has finished, the Mastersingers unanimously vote him the prize, and Eva crowns her knight with a wreath of laurel and myrtle. Pogner inducts Walther into the company of Mastersingers, while the people cheer their beloved Hans Sachs, who has brought about not only the union of the lovers but also the triumph of genuine art.

The Ring of the Nibelungs

(Der Ring des Nibelungen)

INTRODUCTION

The story of *The Ring of the Nibelungs* is based on several ancient myths and legends common to the people of northern Europe who lived in the regions now identified as Iceland, Norway, Sweden, Denmark, and Rhineland Germany. These myths and legends were incorporated into poems in the Old Norse language. The authors of the poems are unknown, and the dates of composition are uncertain—roughly between A.D. 900 and 1200. These poems were gathered into a collection known as the Elder Edda.

From this Elder Edda, in which incidents are unconnected and overlapping, an unknown poet made an integrated poem called the *Nibelungenlied* ("Song of the Nibelungs"). This, the most famous of the medieval German epics, was written probably between A.D. 1190 and 1200.

Snorri Sturlson, an Icelander who lived from 1178 to 1241, made a summary of the Elder Edda, which is known as the Snorra Edda and which is a kind of handbook of the myths and legends of the North.

Also derived from the Elder Edda is the long Volsunga Saga, an epic of the second half of the thirteenth century, written in prose with occasional passages in verse.

In all these versions appear, in one form or another and sometimes with different names, the characters and incidents of Wagner's *The Ring of the Nibelungs.* Wagner, however, concentrated on the figures of Siegfried and Brünnhilde, and produced a much simplified version of the old legends. He unified these by the theme of the ring and the curse upon it, a part of the old legends but rather less important there than in Wagner's treatment.

The more Wagner condensed the old stories, the less realistic they became. For, as details and particulars are omitted in any process whatsoever, the essence of the subject appears. This essence, like a spirit, can then take many different forms and purposes, and through them acquire many meanings.

A common and very real process today may clarify this common procedure of thought and imagination—the refinement of crude oil or petroleum. Gasoline, which the French call *essence,* is the end result of the removal from the original crude oil of the many particulars that conceal it. Crude oil is relatively useless, but gasoline has many uses. In one form, say, it is a solvent of grease; in another, it is a fuel; in another (vapor) it is a source of power. The refiner has, as it were, found the spirit, the element of life, in the original material. He can now make that spirit work for him.

Wagner discovered a spirit, an essence, in his simplification of the old Eddas and Sagas. He saw the whole complicated ancient story as essentially an allegory of power in the world. In *The Ring*, whoever possesses the actual ring also possesses absolute power. The gold of which the ring is made is a symbol of wealth and hence of power.

But, as Lord Acton pointed out, "all power tends to corrupt; and absolute power tends to corrupt absolutely." The problem of *The Ring*, therefore, is the proper use of power. Or, it might be stated as "everyone wants power, but not everyone can use it for his own good or for the good of others."

To use power for the good of others requires love on the part of the user. If he loves others, he also loves himself; hence, power used lovingly is for his own good. The curse on the ring symbolizes the sad fact that few beings, human or divine, can be both powerful and also free from selfish greed. The ring itself destroys everyone who possesses it—for it is always possessed unlawfully, having originally been stolen—and thus eventually destroys the ideal loving order of the world.

Like any other abstraction, *The Ring* is subject to many interpretations—many uses for the benefit of the individual's own philosophy of life. All these possible uses are necessarily subjective, just as one may put gasoline to the use of propelling his automobile or his airplane, or, at the other extreme, leave its usefulness hidden in crude oil. Similarly, one may justify socialism and anarchy by *The Ring*, as the socialist George

Bernard Shaw did, or one may take it merely as a compelling story of human emotions and desires in conflict with one another.

Wagner himself, never very clear in explaining his purposes, seems to have conceived *The Ring* as a colossal drama to express, and impress upon audiences, his belief that only the renunciation of selfish desires can bring happiness to the individual and the world. Love unblemished by possessiveness is the redeeming, freeing factor in life, and everything else must be sacrificed for it.

A brief explanation of the literal world of *The Ring* and of the nature of its characters will perhaps help the reader to understand the action. Wagner based this world on the myths of the Eddas. Like all other myths, these were an objectification of the physical and intellectual experiences of the rather primitive people who developed the myths.

The world is divided into three levels. At the bottom, under the earth, is Nibelheim, a dark region inhabited by dwarfs, the Nibelungs. These are a mean, greedy race, shriveled in every sense of the word, who work unceasingly at materialistic pursuits. Alberich and Mime typify them.

The earth is peopled with giants, a race of great strength, typified by Fafner and Fasolt. The giants think of immediate physical comforts as the best reward for their labor. They are better than the Nibelungs, but they cannot see beyond the intrinsic value of a thing to its use. They are hoarders, content to acquire wealth merely to sleep upon it, never putting it to work for their own benefit or the good of others.

Later, men and women also people the earth. These are either of heroic character if they are of semidivine origin, like Siegmund, Sieglinde, and Siegfried; or base and weak barbarians like Hunding, the Gibichungs, and their clansmen.

In the mountains dwell the gods. These are projections of actual men and women, endowed with superhuman, magical powers due to the use of their intellect. They see beyond the present and work for the future. Owing to the elevation of their habitat, they can see individual things in relation to one another. They embody human laws, but they are above those laws because they live by the spirit rather than the letter of the law. They are immortal, for they are the personifications of ideas, but they can grow old, and they suffer the miseries of human beings.

The scenery is the region around the present city of Worms on the Rhine River. The legendary site of Siegfried's slaying of the dragon is the Siebengebirge opposite Bonn. The time is vague. *The Rhinegold* seems to take place in some primitive period like that before the Flood when, as Genesis 6:4 relates: "There were giants in the earth in those days; and also after that, when the sons of God came in unto the daughters of men, and they bare children to them, the same became mighty men." *The Valkyrie* takes place eons later. The action of *Siegfried* begins about eighteen years after the close of *The Valkyrie. The Twilight of the Gods* follows immediately upon *Siegfried;* its period might be the fifth century A.D., when the legendary Gunther of the *Nibelungenlied* supposedly lived.

The relationships of the characters may be clarified by the following family tree:

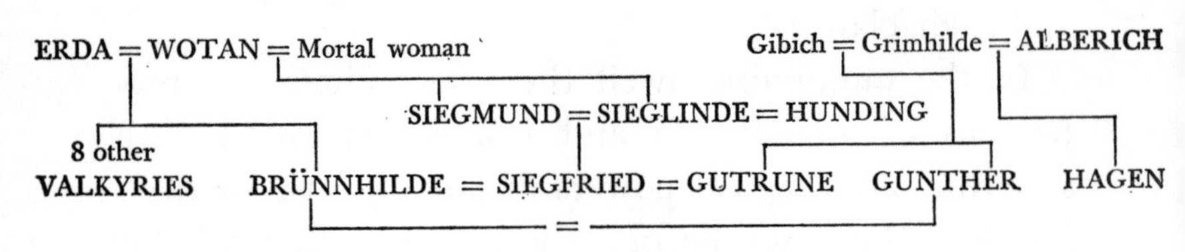

1. The Rhinegold

(*Das Rheingold*)

CHARACTERS

(in order of appearance)

WOGLINDE (Voh-*glin*-da) WELLGUNDE (Vell-*gun*-da) FLOSSHILDE (Floss-*hill*-da)	Rhinemaidens, that is, the tutelary deities of the Rhine River—mermaids, sirens, or nymphs

ALBERICH (*Al*-ber-ish), a Nibelung
WOTAN (*Voh*-tahn), chief of the gods
FRICKA, Wotan's legal wife, the goddess of morality and law
FREIA (*Fry*-ah), Fricka's sister, goddess of youth
DONNER, Freia's brother, god of storm
FROH, Donner's brother, god of good weather
FASOLT, a giant
FAFNER, a giant, Fasolt's brother
LOGE (*Low*-ga), the spirit of fire and of deceit, not quite a god
ERDA (*Air*-da), the primeval goddess of earth, sometimes referred to as WALA, meaning "wisest of beings"
MIME (*Mee*-meh), a Nibelung, Alberich's brother
Nibelung dwarfs

The Rhinegold is not divided into acts, but moves from scene to scene without interruption.

The three beautiful Rhinemaidens are guarding their golden treasure, the Rhinegold, when the hideous dwarf Alberich invades their watery realm to make love to them. They tease him, and unwittingly disclose to him the secret of their treasure, namely, that anyone who could make a ring from their gold would have absolute power over the world. But in order to get the idle gold and put it to use, a person must absolutely renounce love. Since the Rhinemaidens cannot conceive of anyone's doing such a terrible thing, they are sure that their gold is safe. Alberich, however, is so tempted by the gleaming gold and so frustrated by the mermaids' mockery of him that he renounces love and curses it. Then he snatches the gold, and disappears with it, laughing at the despair of the nymphs.

The scene shifts to a flowery meadow in the Rhine valley, where Wotan and Fricka are asleep. As the sun rises, Fricka awakes and sees the towers and battlements of a mountaintop castle gleaming in the early light. This is Valhalla, which Wotan has hired the giants to build as a fortress that is to protect the gods forever. Fricka reminds Wotan that now the castle is finished, he must pay the giants as he promised to do by giving them Freia. Wotan, however, has no intention of keeping his part of the bargain; he is calmly waiting for Loge to get him out of it, as Loge had promised to do.

Loge says that indeed he has tried to find a way for Freia to remain with the gods, but since the giants are in love with her, they will not give her up. "Nothing's so hard," Loge reminds Wotan, "to replace in the heart of a man as woman's sweetness."* But Loge has just heard of Alberich's theft of the Rhinegold, out of which he has made a ring of power. The ring has already brought him vast treasures.

Immediately everyone wants the ring; even Fricka coaxes Wotan to get it. For, as Donner points out, the gods will be Alberich's slaves if the dwarf is allowed to keep the ring. Loge justifies Wotan's seizing the ring from Alberich on the grounds that Alberich himself stole it; therefore it is Wotan's duty to restore it to the Rhinemaidens.

The giants agree to accept Alberich's treasure instead of Freia, for "the magical gold brings eternal youth with its power" just as much as the goddess of youth herself. They take Freia off as a hostage, however, giving Wotan one day in which to ransom her by turning over to the giants the hoard of the Nibelungs.

Wotan and Loge descend to Nibelheim, where Alberich has enslaved all the other dwarfs, including his brother Mime. The clever smith Mime has made a wishing cap, the Tarnhelm, which Alberich now proceeds to take for himself. The resentful Mime tells Wotan and Loge the secret of this cap, whereupon Loge tricks Alberich into demonstrating its power by

* English quotations from *The Ring* are the translation of Stewart Robb.

changing himself into a toad. Loge easily captures the toad, and when Alberich resumes his true shape he is a prisoner of the gods in the upper world.

Wotan sets all of Alberich's hoard as the dwarf's ransom, and Alberich commands his dwarf slaves to bring it. Alberich holds back the ring, but Wotan tears it from his finger. Alberich then puts a terrible curse on the ring so that no one who possesses it shall ever be happy and shall be eventually destroyed.

The giants return Freia, in whose absence the gods have already begun to grow old, and demand that enough of the Nibelung gold completely to cover her must be theirs before they will release her. The piled-up hoard does cover her except for a chink through which her beauty can still be seen. The only treasure left to fill this chink is the Tarnhelm and the ring.

Wotan refuses to yield the ring until Erda rises from the earth to warn him that if he does not surrender it, it will destroy him. Reluctantly Wotan throws it on the heap of gold. Fafner and Fasolt immediately quarrel over which is to have the ring, and Fafner kills his brother to get possession of it. The curse has begun to work.

Having satisfied the giants, Wotan and the other gods now take possession of glorious Valhalla, entering it over a rainbow bridge. Loge lingers behind, reflecting on the trickery with which Valhalla has been secured. Even the wily Loge has been cheated, for he had promised to restore the stolen gold to the Rhinemaidens, whose wailing for their loss Wotan now commands him to silence. Loge laughs cynically as he reflects that the gods are no longer free and so will not be happy in their glorious new abode. Wotan's greed has reduced himself, and through him the other gods, to the level of men.

2. *The Valkyrie*

(Die Walküre)

CHARACTERS

(in order of appearance)

SIEGMUND (*Zeeg*-munt), son of Wotan, who, in the disguise of Wolf the Volsung, had begotten him by a mortal woman

SIEGLINDE (Zee-*glin*-da), Siegmund's twin sister

HUNDING (*Hoon*-ding), Sieglinde's husband

WOTAN

BRÜNNHILDE (Bryn-*hill*-da), Wotan's favorite daughter by Erda

FRICKA

GERHILDE (Gair-*hill*-da) ORTLINDE (Ort-*lin*-da) WALTRAUTE (Vall-*trow*-ta) SCHWERTLEITE (Schvert-*lie*-ta) HELMWIGE (Helm-*veeg*-a) SIEGRUNE (Zee-*groon*-a) GRIMGERDA (Grim-*gert*-a) ROSSWEISSE (Ross-*vie*-sa)	Valkyries, Wotan's other daughters by Erda. Their duty is to bring heroes killed in battle to Valhalla, where the warriors will be restored to life in order to defend the gods from the revenge of Alberich

ACT I

Weaponless, and wounded as the result of a fight to

save a woman from an unwanted marriage, Siegmund flees through the forest in a storm until he comes to shelter, where he claims the ancient right of hospitality. Sieglinde, the mistress of the hut, finds him asleep by the fire, and is strangely attracted to him; when he awakes and is given refreshment, he is similarly affected by her.

Hunding, the master of the hut, returns from hunting and recognizes Siegmund as one of an enemy clan. Hunding observes the laws of hospitality, but tells Siegmund that they must settle their score of blood in the morning.

Sieglinde, having drugged Hunding, returns to tell the guest of the sword that a stranger (actually Wotan) at her marriage feast plunged into the trunk of the tree around which the hut is built. No one has been able to pull it out. She also tells Siegmund of her loveless marriage and of her faith that whoever can pull out the sword will be her truly destined mate who will free her from her miserable life with Hunding.

The storm subsides. The great door at the back of the hut blows open, revealing the beautiful May moonlight. The mutual love of Siegmund and Sieglinde bursts into passion. They recognize that they are the long separated twin children of Wotan, alias Wolf the Volsung, and that the sword is meant for Siegmund, for their father had promised that Siegmund would find a sword when he needed one most. Siegmund's despair over his woeful life turns into exhilaration. He pulls the sword from the tree. The lovers escape together into the spring night.

ACT II

In a rocky mountain pass, Wotan informs Brünnhilde that in the coming fight between Siegmund and Hunding she is to protect Siegmund and bring him to Valhalla. Immediately afterward, however, Fricka arrives to berate Wotan for this disregard of the laws of hospitality, the laws against incest, and the sanctity of marriage.

Reluctantly Wotan recognizes that Fricka is right; he is not free to protect his hero-son Siegmund, who has violated all these laws by eloping with Sieglinde. Nor is Wotan free to recover the ring of power from Fafner; he is bound by a promise.

Meanwhile, Alberich is plotting to get the ring back into his possession, and tempting heroes to become slaves to greed. It is the duty of Brünnhilde to counteract Alberich's influence by encouraging warriors to unselfish deeds of valor, then to bring them to Valhalla to defend it against men who have been corrupted by selfish desires.

By stealing the ring from Alberich, Wotan has deprived himself of freedom, for he must now live in slavish fear of Alberich's revenge. This revenge is soon to come, he knows, for Alberich has bought the love of a woman, and she has borne him a son who will accomplish what Alberich himself cannot. Ironically, Wotan must now destroy his own son, who might have saved him.

Acknowledging that his lust for power has brought about his own imminent destruction, Wotan resigns himself to his fate. He countermands his previous instructions to Brünnhilde, and orders her not to protect Siegmund.

When Siegmund and the exhausted, hysterical Sieglinde appear in their flight from Hunding's vengeance, Brünnhilde confronts Siegmund with Wotan's decision that he must perish. Siegmund, however, defies this judgment so boldly, and so convincingly demonstrates his love for Sieglinde, that Brünnhilde decides to do what Wotan really wishes her to do. To her, this is clearly a situation where an individual's value must be put before a general law. In the fight between Siegmund and Hunding, Brünnhilde, therefore, protects Siegmund with her shield.

Wotan, however, must be true to his promise to Fricka. With his spear, which symbolizes faithfulness to one's word, he shatters the sword he had planted in the tree—the needed weapon of courage which would have liberated Siegmund from the fetters of morality and made him a brave, independent hero. Hunding kills Siegmund, but Wotan destroys Hunding as a cowardly slave to an arbitrary law.

ACT III

On a high rock in a fir forest, the eight Valkyries are gathering after a day of galloping through the air bearing slain warriors on their saddlebows to Valhalla. As they are tethering their horses, Brünnhilde joins them on her horse Grani, bringing not a warrior but the desperate Sieglinde. Wotan, in a towering rage over Brünnhilde's disobedience of his expressed command, is furiously pursuing her to punish her.

Brünnhilde gives Sieglinde the fragments of Siegmund's broken sword, and sends her for safety into the forest with the comforting prophecy that the child she has conceived by Siegmund will be the greatest of all heroes and is to be named Siegfried.

The Valkyries try to hide Brünnhilde from Wotan's wrath, but Brünnhilde bravely steps forward to receive her punishment. She is to be deprived of her immortality, cast out of Valhalla, and put into a sleep. Any man who finds her can have her.

Pleading not to be so disgraced, Brünnhilde reminds her father that she had done only what Wotan truly wished her to do, and so she has saved him from the shame of having to yield to Fricka. Wotan's reply is that Brünnhilde let her love for Siegmund overcome her sense of duty; consequently she is no longer fit to be Wotan's confidante and fellow worker for the good of the world. Brünnhilde then argues that by shaming her, Wotan is shaming himself. Deeply moved by his love for Brünnhilde, Wotan agrees to soften her punishment. He will surround her sleeping form with a wall of fire and provide that only one more free than he shall brave the flames and awaken her.

Tenderly Wotan says a long farewell to his beloved daughter, and kisses her into her slumber. He summons Loge to surround the rock with fire, and vanishes through the flames, foretelling that "he who fears the point of Wotan's spear shall never penetrate the flames."

3. Siegfried

CHARACTERS

(in order of appearance)

MIME

SIEGFRIED, son of Siegmund and Sieglinde, and Wotan's grandson

THE WANDERER, Wotan dressed in a long cloak and a broad-brimmed drooping hat, and using his spear as a staff

ALBERICH

FAFNER, in the form of a dragon, into which he has changed himself in order to guard the gold of the Nibelungs, the Tarnhelm, and the ring

A FOREST BIRD

ERDA

BRÜNNHILDE

ACT I

The spiteful, treacherous Nibelung dwarf Mime is working at his smithy, trying to mend Siegmund's sword Nothung (Needful), for Mime knows that only that weapon can kill the dragon who guards the Nibelung treasure which Mime is determined to repossess.

Siegfried, now a powerful adolescent, loathes the sniveling Mime, who, he knows, cannot be his real father, as Mime has led him to believe. For Mime had found the dying Sieglinde in the forest, rescued her infant son, and also the fragments of Siegmund's sword. Siegfried teases Mime cruelly, and beats him for his inability to forge the sword which Siegfried knows is his own rightful weapon. Once he has the sword, Siegfried can be free of Mime and can then go about fulfilling the destiny he senses is his.

Wotan, disguised as a wanderer, asks hospitality of Mime. From him Mime learns that only the hero who does not know what fear is will be able to forge the sword. Mime recognizes that the person is Siegfried, to whom Mime has taught everything except the meaning of fear. Once he has forged the sword, Siegfried will kill the dragon and get the treasure Mime covets, and, as Wotan darkly hints, will then kill Mime.

When Siegfried returns from the forest, Mime tries to teach him fear by describing the dragon, but Siegfried welcomes the idea of encountering this beast. Impatient with Mime's fumbling delays, Siegfried determines to forge the sword himself. He files the pieces to shreds, melts them, pours the liquid steel into a mold, tempers it, and with the reconstituted sword splits Mime's anvil in two. But all the time Siegfried has been working at the forge, the cowering Mime has been plotting to poison him as soon as Siegfried has slain the dragon and got the hoard, the Tarnhelm, and the ring.

ACT II

Before daylight Alberich crouches by the cave of Fafner, the giant turned dragon, keeping watch over the guardian of the treasure that would give Alberich world mastery again, eagerly anticipating the day when the dragon will be killed.

The Wanderer interrupts Alberich's brooding. Alberich recognizes him as Wotan, taunts him with having been trapped by his own trickery, and warns him that if he tries to cheat Fafner as he once cheated Alberich, his power will crumble. Wotan replies that he has no intention of getting the ring, but that Mime has, and Mime at that very moment is bringing the hero who will kill the dragon. Alberich wakes Fafner to tell him of his approaching death, which Alberich says he can prevent if only Fafner will give him the ring at once. Fafner refuses, and goes back to sleep.

As day breaks, Mime and Siegfried arrive before Fafner's cave. Again Mime tries to arouse fear in Siegfried by describing the dragon, but Siegfried only chases the dwarf away, and lies down in the shade of a linden tree. Wishing to know what the birds are saying, Siegfried fashions a pipe with which he futilely tries to imitate their song and thus be able to converse with them. In disgust he tries his silver hunting horn as a better instrument.

Siegfried's horn blast awakens Fafner. The dragon tries to terrify the youth, but Siegfried only laughs, and at an opportune moment, plunges his sword straight into the dragon's heart. Dying, Fafner warns Siegfried of Mime's plot against him, and expires.

Some of the dragon's blood has spattered on to Siegfried's hand, burning it like acid. Siegfried licks his hand, and at once discovers that he can understand what the forest bird is saying. The bird tells him of the treasure and of the Tarnhelm and the ring and their wonderful properties. Siegfried goes to get them from Fafner's cave.

Mime and Alberich are quarreling over which of them shall have the treasure, when Siegfried returns from the cave with the Tarnhelm and the ring—all he seems to want of the hoard. Mime tries to wheedle them away from him, but, thanks to the dragon's blood, Siegfried can read Mime's thoughts and also understand the bird's warning that the drink Mime is offering him is poison. Filled with new loathing for the evil dwarf, Siegfried swiftly kills Mime with the sword. Alberich, in hiding, laughs mockingly at how his curse on the ring has claimed another victim, and foresees that Siegfried himself is doomed by possessing it.

Again Siegfried rests under the linden tree, envying the birds their lovemaking. Love now is what he wants, for, like fear, he has never known it. The bird tells Siegfried of the sleeping Brünnhilde, who can be wakened only by the man who knows not fear. Siegfried recognizes that it is he who is destined to possess this splendid bride, and gleefully follows the bird who proceeds to guide him to the flame-encircled rock.

ACT III

In the depth of the forest, Wotan the Wanderer, seeing that he has set in motion a chain of events that he cannot control, summons Erda to advise him "how to check this rolling wheel." The all-wise Erda claims to know nothing; she merely hints that redeeming wisdom will come to her daughter Brünnhilde. Finally Wotan discloses to Erda that, for the good of the world, he will allow the gods to perish. He wills that Siegfried, who is freer than the gods, shall wed Brünnhilde and that from them shall spring a new race that will make a new and better world.

When Siegfried, on his way to the flame-girt rock, encounters the Wanderer, Wotan tries to deter him. Siegfried sees him only as Siegmund's enemy who shattered the sword of courage. With that sword, Siegfried now shatters Wotan's spear on which are written the covenants that bind men to the will of the gods.

Siegfried's fearless act is the climactic moment of *The Ring*. He has rendered Wotan powerless. His breaking of Wotan's spear symbolizes the beginning of a new world order in which men will be free from superstitious worship of gods who are no better than themselves. Men can now make their own destiny, relying on their own integrity for whatever guiding and controlling laws they may need.

Blowing his horn triumphantly, Siegfried bursts through the fiery barrier and discovers the sleeping Brünnhilde. As he wonderingly removes the armor from the first woman he has ever seen, he exclaims, "This is no man"—unfortunately one of opera's most inane remarks. The love he feels he mistakes for the fear Mime described.

The awakened Brünnhilde gazes on Siegfried with rapture and longing. Then she remembers what she has lost, and begs him not to possess her. Siegfried breaks down her defenses. Finally Brünnhilde laughingly yields to him, willing to sacrifice her immortality and the glories of Valhalla, and to see the old gods perish, so long as throughout the darkness to come Siegfried's star will shine for her until the dawn of the new day that both of them have been destined to create.

4. The Twilight of the Gods

(*Die Götterdämmerung*)

CHARACTERS

(in order of appearance)

THE THREE NORNS, the Fates, daughters of Erda
BRÜNNHILDE
SIEGFRIED
GUNTHER (*Goon*-tare), chief of the Gibichungs, a clan of the Rhineland, son of Queen Grimhilde and Gibich
HAGEN (*Hah*-ghenn), his half-brother, son of Queen Grimhilde and Alberich
GUTRUNE (Goot-*roon*-a), Gunther's sister
WALTRAUTE, a Valkyrie, Brünnhilde's sister
ALBERICH
WOGLINDE
WELLGUNDE
FLOSSHILDE
Vassals of Gunther; servingwomen of Gutrune

PROLOGUE

On Brünnhilde's rock, the Norns are weaving the rope of the world's destiny by night, when they find that they have lost their power to see into the future.

The rope breaks, symbolizing that the old order of the world is ending.

As the sun rises, Brünnhilde sends Siegfried on new adventures, giving him her horse Grani. Siegfried gives her the ring.

ACT I, Scene 1

In a great hall on the banks of the Rhine, Hagen schemes with his half-brother and half-sister to marry Gunther to Brünnhilde and Gutrune to Siegfried in order to perpetuate the line of the renowned Gibichungs. This family conference reveals that Gunther is a weak fool who mistakes Hagen's craftiness for intelligence, that Hagen is a villain, and that Gutrune is a gentle, guileless creature who does what she is told without asking the purpose.

When Siegfried's horn is heard, Hagen bids Gutrune to welcome this distinguished guest with a drink into which she is to put a drug that will deprive Siegfried of his memory. Ironically, Siegfried drinks to Brünnhilde, whom a moment later he completely forgets. Immediately he falls in love with Gutrune. Gunther promises him Gutrune as a wife if Siegfried will capture Brünnhilde for him. Siegfried agrees to this; he will assume Gunther's form through the Tarnhelm's magic. Siegfried and Gunther perform the primitive ritual that makes them blood brothers, and set out together for Brünnhilde's fire-encircled rock.

Left alone, Hagen muses that Siegfried will bring Brünnhilde back for Gunther, but for Hagen he will bring a far more valuable prize—the ring, with which Hagen will destroy every one of the group he secretly hates.

ACT I, Scene 2

Brünnhilde is thinking lovingly of Siegfried, and kissing the ring, when Waltraute gallops through the air to tell her everything that happened during her long sleep. Wotan, his spear shattered, now sits in silent grief over the loss of Brünnhilde, his power gone. The gods have grown old. Waltraute begs Brünnhilde to give the ring back to its rightful owners, the Rhine-maidens, and thus end the sorrow of the gods. Brünnhilde refuses to part with the pledge of Siegfried's love.

Siegfried, in Gunther's form and with the Tarnhelm covering his face, breaks through the fire and claims Brünnhilde as a bride. Utterly confused and terrified, Brünnhilde shows the ring, trusting in its power to protect her from this unwelcome intruder. Siegfried tears it from her finger as his—that is, Gunther's—prize. They go into the cave together, Siegfried swearing on his sword that he will not betray his blood brother Gunther with the bride he has promised to bring him; the sword will lie between them.

ACT II

Half-asleep, Hagen guards the entrance to the Gibichungs' hall. Alberich whispers to him that Siegfried, not Wotan, is now their enemy; that Siegfried, being motivated by love, does not know the hateful power of the ring; and that Hagen must get the ring from Siegfried, even if he has to murder the innocent hero. Hagen swears that he will do his father's bidding.

The sky lightens, and Siegfried, who has flown back through the Tarnhelm's power, appears in his own form to announce to Hagen that everything went as planned and that Gunther and Brünnhilde are even now coming down the Rhine in a boat. Hagen summons Gunther's vassals to prepare a wedding feast for their chief, and for Siegfried and Gutrune.

As soon as Brünnhilde sees Siegfried, she almost faints with astonishment, for, of course, Siegfried does not recognize her, owing to the drink of forgetfulness. As she sees the ring on Siegfried's finger, the truth begins to dawn on her. Siegfried's total inability to explain how he came by the ring, except that he got it from the dragon he killed, leads Hagen to accuse him of treachery.

Furious at the way she has been betrayed, Brünnhilde calls on the gods to witness that she is Siegfried's wife and that no sword lay between them in the cave on the fire-ringed rock.

The vassals demand that Siegfried swear that his story is the true one; otherwise, they will kill him as a traitor to their chief, his blood brother. Siegfried takes the oath on Hagen's spear, swearing that if he has lied, then may that spear strike him dead.

Brünnhilde breaks through the circle of vassals witnessing Siegfried's oath, tears his hand away from the spearhead, places her own there, and swears that Siegfried has lied and may that very spear strike him down.

Siegfried advises Gunther that Brünnhilde is hysterical and needs a good rest. He gaily goes off with Gutrune to their wedding feast.

Left alone with Hagen and Gunther, Brünnhilde begs for an explanation, for she has given all her powers of divination to Siegfried, who now has cast her off and so shamed her that she wishes to kill herself. Hagen offers to dispose of Siegfried for her, but Brünnhilde contemptuously informs him that one flash of the hero's eye would disarm him. Unfortunately for her, she has made Siegfried invulnerable—except, she remembers, for his back, on which she worked no spell, knowing that he would never turn it to any foe. Grimly Hagen responds: "My spear knows where to strike."

Horrified at the thought of being party to the murder of his blood brother, Gunther refuses to join the plot. Hagen, however, persuades him that Siegfried's death is obligatory to wipe out Gunther's shame. To spare Gutrune, it will be made to seem a hunting accident.

ACT III, Scene 1

Siegfried has lost his fellow hunters and the track of the game, and is wandering alone by the shore of the Rhine. The Rhinemaidens surface, and offer to put him back on the right track if he will give them the ring he is wearing. When he refuses, they tease him for being stingy, and accuse him of being afraid of his wife. At last he offers them the ring, but they refuse to take it until after it has worked its curse on him. That day, they tell him, he shall die.

Hagen and the hunters catch up with Siegfried, and they all sit down to rest and eat. As Siegfried is telling them of his youth with Mime, the slaying of the dragon, and his gift of understanding the birds, Hagen gives him a drink that restores his memory. Siegfried goes on to tell of his wakening and winning of Brünnhilde. Gunther at last understands the situation, but he is too late to stop Hagen from plunging his spear into Siegfried's back.

ACT III, Scene 2

The vassals bear Siegfried's body on his shield to the courtyard of the Gibichungs' Hall, and lay it on a funeral pyre. Gunther accuses Hagen of the murder, which Hagen admits, claiming the ring as his reward for avenging Siegfried's false oath. Gunther protests that the ring is rightfully his, but Hagen kills him before he can get it. Hagen then reaches for the ring, but is frightened off by the dead man's hand rising threateningly.

Gutrune confesses her part in the tragedy—the drink of forgetfulness—and curses Hagen. After learning from Brünnhilde that she never was Siegfried's true love, Gutrune swoons on Gunther's body.

Brünnhilde orders the vassals to pile the pyre high. She sings the praises of the hero she has lost. In betraying her, she now understands, Siegfried did what Wotan willed, namely, to take the curse of the ring upon himself. Now Wotan and all the gods shall perish through her revenge. She orders Loge to enter Valhalla at last.

Brünnhilde takes the ring from Siegfried's finger, and promises it to the Rhinemaidens. She prophesies that the fire which is about to consume her will purge the world of the curse on the ring. She calls for Grani, her horse. Then she flings a torch on the funeral pyre. As it blazes up, she leaps on Grani's back and rides into the flames, shouting to Siegfried that she is joining him in deathless love.

The fire rises high, and swallows her. Then as the blaze dies down, the Rhine rises and quenches the embers. The Rhinemaidens are riding on its waves.

As Hagen sees them, he flings himself into the water, exclaiming, "The ring is mine!" Woglinde and Wellgunde seize him and drag him down to the depths of the river, while Flosshilde swims away on the surface, holding aloft the long lost ring.

In the smoky sky a red glow appears. It reveals Valhalla with the gods resignedly waiting for the flames that will presently devour the splendid abode. The gods are gone, and with them the envy and fear that lay between men and them. The world, however, remains, purified by the redeeming love of Brünnhilde's self-sacrifice. Love is the force that thereafter will govern the world.

CHARACTERS

(in order of appearance)

GURNEMANZ (*Goor*-neh-mants), a veteran knight of the Holy Grail
KUNDRY (*Koon*-dree), a mysterious woman who seems to represent the essence of womanhood since time began
AMFORTAS, guardian of the Holy Grail
PARSIFAL
TITUREL, Amfortas' aged father
KLINGSOR, a sorcerer
Knights, squires, and pages of the Holy Grail. Flower Maidens

The scene is the sanctuary of the Holy Grail on Monsalvat, Spain (see p. 233, note), and the region around it. The time is presumably the early Middle Ages.

BACKGROUND

The Holy Grail figures in many of the poems that make up the medieval cycles of romance, among which is Wolfram von Eschenbach's *Parzifal* of the early thirteenth century, Wagner's principal source.

Originally a pagan fertility-symbol, the Grail eventually was transformed into the cup that contained the wine which Christ drank at the Last Supper, when He instituted the ritual of Communion, saying: "This is my blood which is shed for many for the forgiveness of sins" (Matthew 26:28). It was also identified with the vessel that caught Christ's blood after His side was pierced by Longinus' lance as He hung on the cross. The lance, also originally a pagan fertility-symbol, the mistletoe, became joined with the Grail as Christian symbols of spiritual rebirth and renewal from the "death" of sin. For Christ's redeeming blood, shed for mankind, renews man's life by restoring his spirit.

In the nineteenth-century revival of the medieval legends, the Holy Grail acquired a mystical significance. It came to symbolize the essential meaning of Communion, one of the mysteries of the Christian religion. Through Communion, the spirit of God becomes one with man's by the mediation of Christ's sacrificial blood. Consequently, in *Parsifal,* Wagner makes the Holy Grail represent the mystical healing-power of Communion on body and soul.

According to legend, an angel gave the Grail and the lance for safekeeping to the holy Titurel, who built the temple of the Grail and organized a company of pure knights to guard the treasures and exemplify their healing, comforting power by doing good works throughout the world. Titurel's son, Amfortas, however, allowed himself to be seduced by the pagan sorcerer Klingsor and Klingsor's temptresses. By that sin, Amfortas lost the sacred lance to Klingsor. With it, Klingsor gave Amfortas a grievous wound. By this story, Wagner intends to say that the man who has sinned by defiling his original purity suffers ever afterward as if from a painful wound that will not heal until his sin is washed away by Christ's forgiveness.

ACT I

Amfortas is being brought from the temple of the Grail to a nearby lake in which he will bathe in order to relieve the pain of his wound. Old Gurnemanz explains to two young squires (apprentice knights) that the water will not cure the keeper of the Grail; only a "blameless fool made wise through pity" can do that. The knights are praying for such a one to make his appearance.

In wild and ragged clothing Kundry reels into the glade by the lake with balsam that she has brought from Arabia as a salve for Amfortas' wound. The motifs in the music make it clear that it was Kundry, the unwilling slave of Klingsor, who tempted Amfortas to sin—an act for which she now does penance by seeking all over the world for a balm that will heal the wound Amfortas got as a result of yielding to her temptation.

Klingsor, Gurnemanz tells the squires, had hoped to be a guardian knight of the Grail, but was too sinful to achieve that ambition. In revenge, Klingsor stole the sacred lance, the possession of which makes him a constant threat to the pure knights. Klingsor has also transformed the barren country opposite Monsalvat into an enchanted garden into which he entices the knights of the Grail in order to rob them of their purity.

Suddenly a wounded wild swan falls to the ground, horrifying everyone in this peaceful realm, where all life is protected as sacred. The knights bring in Parsifal, who has shot the bird without being aware that he was doing wrong. When Gurnemanz reproaches him, Parsifal, overcome with grief, breaks his bow and arrows and resolves never to kill again.

Kundry, who knows more than Parsifal does about his origins, relates that he was born posthumously to a woman who raised him in isolation from human society and in total ignorance of the competitive ways of men so that her son would not die in warfare as his father did. Learning from Kundry that his mother has recently died, Parsifal almost faints from sorrow.

This bit of biography somewhat clarifies the term, "the guileless fool," which is often applied to Parsifal in the course of the drama. He is a "fool" only in the sense that he is utterly unsophisticated; he is "guileless" because he is not "of the world" (see Jesus' prayer of intercession for the righteous, John 17:15-16).

Seeing Amfortas being carried back from the lake,

Parsifal inquires about the Grail. Gurnemanz senses that Parsifal may be the one destined to heal Amfortas. He takes Parsifal to the ritual in the Temple, where the boy may witness the power of the Grail.

The scene changes to the sanctuary of the Grail. Age has forced the holy Titurel to turn over the guardianship of the relic and the conducting of its ritual to Amfortas. Titurel commands Amfortas to uncover the sacred chalice so that it may transform the bread and wine, the symbols of communion, into the spirit-renewing—hence, life-renewing—body and blood of Christ. Amfortas is reluctant to do so, for the Grail only tortures him because of his sin. The exaltation that Amfortas experiences as he again sees the Grail makes the blood burst from his wound, and he has to be carried from the hall as the knights take the holy repast of bread and wine which the Grail has consecrated.

Parsifal, unable to comprehend what he has seen, is chased out of the hall by the disappointed Gurnemanz. Wagner's implication is that Parsifal must acquire wisdom in order to understand the meaning of the Grail and be able to serve it.

ACT II

From the tower of his castle, where he is plotting evil sorcery before a magic mirror, Klingsor summons

Kundry, who has been in one of her cataleptic trances. Like Erda, the all-wise earth goddess of *The Ring*, Kundry spends much of her time in a state of suspended animation.

Klingsor orders Kundry to seduce Parsifal, whose purity is the greatest challenge Klingsor has yet encountered in his evil campaign against the knights of the Grail. Kundry resists Klingsor's command, but his magic compels her to his will.

The dark castle vanishes, and in its place appears a beautiful sunny garden, over the wall of which Parsifal has just leaped. He carries a bloody sword, for he has had to fight his way through the castle's defenders, former knights of the Grail whom Klingsor's maidens have seduced. Apparently it is all right for Parsifal to kill these wayward human beings.

Klingsor's maidens, dressed and perfumed as flowers, offer all their charms to Parsifal, but he repulses them rudely—to their considerable disgust.

Seeing that the Flower Maidens are getting nowhere, Kundry herself appears, this time wide-awake and in ravishing attire. When Kundry tells Parsifal that his leaving his mother literally broke that poor woman's heart, he is overcome with the painful thought that he had thus caused another person grief. His remorse awakens love in him, for he suddenly understands that love springs from a recognition of, and an identity with, another person's feelings—a kind of communion.

This discovery begins the transformation of Parsifal from the "guileless fool" to the man "made wise through pity."

Kundry, however, plays upon Parsifal's new awareness of love by pressing a long kiss upon his lips. Her gesture causes him intense pain. It dawns on Parsifal that he has just been wounded as Amfortas was.

He feels complete sympathy with the suffering guardian of the Grail. It was not, he sees, Amfortas' human yielding to sensuous love that afflicted him, but his betrayal of the idea of self-sacrificing love—the divine love Christ represents. Parsifal now conceives his mission as the salvation of Amfortas by renouncing any love that might bring pleasure to himself in favor of love that seeks no reward. This is the climactic moment of the drama.

Kundry just laughs* at Parsifal, and vigorously renews her extraordinarily persuasive attempts to make him yield to her. Instead he rebukes her and urges her to repent.

Desperate, Kundry calls Klingsor to her aid. Klingsor hurls the sacred lance at Parsifal, but it merely hovers over Parsifal's head. Parsifal grasps it and makes

* Earlier in her existence as the eternal woman, Kundry had laughed at Christ on His way to Calvary. Hence she must wander until Christ's Second Coming. Wagner implies that Kundry, among other things, is the legendary Wandering Jew—one of the mockers of whom Christ said: "There be some standing here, which shall not taste of death till they see the Son of Man coming in his kingdom" (Matthew 16:28; Mark 9:1).

the sign of the Cross with it. Immediately the castle and the garden fall to ruin. Carrying the lance, Parsifal begins his long search for Amfortas and the Grail—meaning the long spiritual experiences he must undergo before being ready to work his healing mission and achieve perfection.

ACT III

Years later, on a shining Good Friday morning, Parsifal returns to the domain of the Grail, where he finds Gurnemanz, now an aged hermit, and Kundry. Kundry has apparently been asleep all this time, but now she awakes and declares that she will thereafter devote all her efforts to service.

Parsifal's quest has sobered him and made him wise and compassionate as a result of all the suffering he has seen. In his absence, as he learns from the informative Gurnemanz, Amfortas has refused to uncover the Grail. Deprived of its life-renewing power, the knights have grown old and tired, and no longer pursue their rescuing missions. Titurel has died and is to be buried that very day.

Parsifal is convinced that this sad state of affairs at Monsalvat is due to his own delay in returning. He faints from remorse, but is revived by water from the sacred spring near Gurnemanz' hut. Kundry bathes his feet, soothes them with ointment that she happens to be keeping in her bosom, and dries them with her hair.*

These ministrations are to prepare Parsifal for the new role he is to assume—Keeper of the Grail in place of Amfortas—thanks to his having brought back the lance to Monsalvat. Gurnemanz anoints Parsifal's head with the rest of Kundry's vial of oil. Parsifal then baptizes Kundry, and finally gives her the kiss she wanted so badly in the enchanted garden. But this is the chaste kiss of pity and forgiveness—Kundry's initiation into the fellowship of the redeemed.

Gurnemanz and Kundry dress Parsifal in the armor and robes of a knight of the Grail, and take him to Titural's funeral in the sanctuary. Amfortas, yearning for death, refuses to uncover the life-sustaining Grail when the knights order him to do so as his duty. As Amfortas is raving, Parsifal steps forward with the lance and touches Amfortas' wound with its point. Amfortas is instantaneously healed.

Parsifal then uncovers the Grail and consecrates the bread and wine, as Kundry sinks lifeless at his feet. Her curse of wandering is over, for the compassionate love of Christ has come again to the world in the person of Parsifal.

* Kundry now seems to represent the repentant Mary Magdalene (John 12:3).

Chronology

1813 Wilhelm Richard Wagner born, Leipzig, May 22. Karl Friedrich Wagner dies, November 22.

1814 Joanna Rosina Wagner marries Ludwig Geyer, August 14. Family moves to Dresden.

1821 Ludwig Geyer dies, September 30. Dispersal of family.

1827 Wagner rejoins family in Leipzig. Attends St. Nicholas School. *Leubald and Adelaide* finished.

1830 Wagner's Overture in B flat major performed, December 25, and greeted with derision.

1831 Wagner enters Leipzig University, February 23. Studies composition with Theodor Weinlig.

1832 Symphony in C major completed, March. Libretto and first act music for *The Wedding,* later abandoned.

1833 With Würzburg Theater, January–April. *The Fairies* completed.

1834 Joins Magdeburg theatrical company at Lauchstädt. Meets Minna Planer.

1836 *Forbidden Love* produced, Magdeburg, March

29. Wagner goes to Königsberg, July 7. Marries Minna Planer, November 24.

1837 Minna elopes with merchant, May. Wagner conceives *Rienzi.* Appointed musical director of Riga Theater. Reunited with Minna, October 19.

1839 Escape from Riga, June. Arrives Paris, September 17.

1840 *Rienzi* finished, November 19.

1841 *Rienzi* accepted by Dresden Court Theater, June. *The Flying Dutchman* finished, September; accepted by Berlin Opera, November.

1842 Wagner leaves Paris for Dresden, April 7. *Rienzi* produced, October 20.

1843 *The Flying Dutchman* produced, January 2. Wagner appointed royal conductor of Dresden Opera, February 2.

1845 *Tannhäuser* finished, April 13. Sketch for *The Mastersingers,* summer; abandoned for work on *Lohengrin. Tannhäuser* produced, October 19.

1847 *Lohengrin* music finished, August 28.

1848 Libretto of "Siegfried's Death" finished, November 28.

1849 Wagner active in revolution of May 3–10. Escapes to Weimar, May 13. Settles in Zürich, June.

1850 Affair with Jessie Laussot. *Lohengrin* produced by Franz Liszt in Weimar, August 28. First meeting with Mathilde Wesendonck, October.

1851 *Opera and Drama* finished, February 16. Libretto of "Young Siegfried" finished, June 24. Annuity from Julie Ritter, November.

1852 Intimate friendship with Mathilde Wesendonck begins. Libretto of *The Valkyrie* finished, July 1. Libretto of *The Rhinegold* finished, November 3. "Young Siegfried" and "Siegfried's Death" converted into *Siegfried* and *The Twilight of the Gods* respectively, end of year.

1854 Music of *The Rhinegold* completed, May 28.

1856 Music of *The Valkyrie* completed, March 23.

1857 Wagner moves into the Asyl, April 29. Poem of *Tristan and Isolde* begun, August. First meeting with Cosima von Bülow, October.

1858 Wagner leaves the Asyl, August 17, and goes to Venice.

1859 Wagner leaves Venice for Lucerne, March 23. Completes music of *Tristan and Isolde,* early August. Leaves for Paris, September. Minna rejoins him, November.

1861 *Tannhäuser* performed at Paris Opéra, March 13.

1862 Libretto of *The Mastersingers* finished, January 25. Wagner settles in Biebrich, February. Granted full amnesty (partially awarded in 1860) for revolutionary activities in 1849, allowing him to return to Saxony, March 28. Final parting from Minna, November. Moves to Vienna, November 15.

1864 Escapes from creditors in Vienna, March 23. Receives invitation to visit King Ludwig II of Bavaria, May 3; meets Ludwig in Munich, May 4.

1865 *Tristan and Isolde* produced in Munich, June 10. Wagner temporarily exiled from Bavaria; departs for Switzerland, December 10.

1866 Minna Wagner dies, January 25. Wagner settles in Geneva; joined by Cosima von Bülow. Moves into Triebschen, near Lucerne, April 4.

1867 *The Mastersingers* finished, October 24.

1869 Siegfried Wagner born, June 6.

1870 Wagner conceives idea of national theater in Bayreuth, March 5. Cosima divorced by Hans von Bülow, July 18; marries Wagner, August 25. *Siegfried Idyll* performed for Cosima's birthday, December 25.

1871 *Siegfried* finished, February 5. Wagner announces plan for Bayreuth festival, May 12.

1872 Leaves Triebschen for Bayreuth, February. Cornerstone of Festspielhaus laid, May 22. Wagner begins fund raising for festival.

1874 Financing of Bayreuth festival assured through loan from King Ludwig II; contract signed, February 26. Wagner takes possession of Wahnfried, April 28. *The Twilight of the Gods* finished, November 21.

1876 Rehearsals of *The Ring* at Bayreuth begin, June 3. First cycle of performances, August 13–17, continuing through August 30.

1877 Wagner conducts concert series in London, May–June, in order to reduce Bayreuth deficit. His health begins to fail.

1882 *Parsifal* finished, January 13. First performance, Bayreuth, July 30. Wagner suffers severe heart attack, August 31. Leaves for Venice, September 14.

1883 Wagner dies in Venice, February 13. Buried at Wahnfried, February 18.

Bibliography

The number of books and articles about Richard Wagner and his works, not to mention the biographies, memoirs, and letters of persons connected with him, which often contain interesting and important data about him, reaches into the thousands. Consequently, there are listed below only works in English, or translated into English, of relatively recent date and more or less easily obtainable in public libraries in the United States or in bookstores.

The complete edition of Wagner's prose works, translated into English by W. Ashton Ellis, is listed below. A judicious and readable selection from those difficult works is that edited by Goldman and Sprinchorn (see below), which should be adequate for the casual reader.

There are many collections of Wagner's letters, but probably no complete one. Perhaps the most interesting of those which have been translated into English are the ones edited by Wilhelm Altmann, and by John N. Burk (the Burrell Collection), listed below.

WAGNER'S WORKS

The Librettos of the Wagner Operas. New York: Crown, 1938.

My Life. New York: Dodd, Mead, 1911.

Richard Wagner's Prose Works, translated by William Ashton Ellis. London: K. Paul, Trench & Trübner, 1892–99, 8 vols.

The Ring of the Nibelung, translated by Stewart Robb. New York: E. P. Dutton, 1960.

Tristan and Isolde, translated by Stewart Robb. New York: E. P. Dutton, 1965.

Altmann, Wilhelm, editor. *Letters of Richard Wagner,* translated by M. M. Bozman. London: Dent, 1927, 2 vols.

Burrell, Mary. *Letters of Richard Wagner: the Burrell Collection,* edited with notes by John N. Burk. New York: Macmillan, 1950.

Goldman, Albert and Evert Sprinchorn, editors. *Wagner on Music and Drama, a Compendium of Richard Wagner's Prose Works.* New York: E. P. Dutton, 1964.

BIOGRAPHY AND CRITICISM

Bertram, Werner. *A Royal Recluse: Memories of Ludwig II of Bavaria,* translated by Margaret McDonough. Munich: Martin Herpich & Son, 1936.

Burrell, Mary. *Richard Wagner—His Life and Works from 1813 to 1834*. London: priv. pr., 1898.

Chamberlain, Houston S. *Richard Wagner*, translated by G. A. Hight. Philadelphia: J. B. Lippincott, 1897.

Donington, Robert. *Wagner's "Ring" and Its Symbols*. New York: St. Martin's Press, 1963.

Ellis, W. Ashton. *The Life of Richard Wagner*. London: K. Paul, Trench, Trübner, 1900–6, 5 vols.

Finck, Henry T. *Wagner and His Works*. New York: C. Scribner's Sons, 1907, 2 vols.

Gautier, Judith. *Wagner at Home*, translated by E. D. Massie. London: Mills & Boon, 1910.

Gilman, Lawrence. *Wagner's Operas*. New York: Farrar & Rinehart, 1937.

Gollancz, Victor. *The Ring at Bayreuth*. New York: E. P. Dutton, 1967.

Hadow, W. H. *Richard Wagner*. London: T. Butterworth, 1934.

Hight, George A. *Richard Wagner: a Critical Biography*. London: Arrowsmith, 1925, 2 vols.

Jacobs, Robert L. *Wagner*. New York: Macmillan (Collier Books), 1962.

Kapp, Julius. *The Women in Wagner's Life*. London: George Routledge & Sons, 1932.

Moulin-Eckart, Richard. *Cosima Wagner*, translated by Catherine Allison Phillips. New York: Alfred A. Knopf, 1931, 2 vols.

Newman, Ernest. *Fact and Fiction about Wagner.* London: Cassell, 1931.
———. *The Life of Richard Wagner.* New York: Alfred A. Knopf, 1933–46, 4 vols.
———. *Wagner as Man and Artist.* London: Victor Gollancz, 1963.
———. *The Wagner Operas.* New York: Alfred A. Knopf, 1949.
Panofsky, Walter. *Wagner, a Pictorial Biography.* New York: Viking Press, 1964.
Pourtalès, Guy de. *Richard Wagner,* translated by Lewis May. New York: Harper & Brothers, 1932.
Rayner, Robert M. *Wagner and "Die Meistersinger."* New York: Oxford University Press, 1940.
Shaw, George Bernard. *The Perfect Wagnerite, a Commentary on the Nibelung's Ring.* New York: Dover, 1967.
Skelton, Geoffrey. *Wagner at Bayreuth: Experiment and Tradition.* New York: George Braziller, 1967.
Wallace, William. *Richard Wagner as He Lived.* New York: Harper & Brothers, 1925.

Index